# color *by* color
## PLANT DIRECTORY

# color *by* color
## PLANT DIRECTORY

LUCY HUNTINGTON
WITH DAVID SQUIRE

CHARTWELL
BOOKS, INC.

First published in 2004 by
CHARTWELL BOOKS INC.
A Division of Book Sales Inc.
114 Northfield Avenue
Edison, New Jersey 08837

ISBN 0-7858-1940-1

This book was conceived, designed and produced by
THE IVY PRESS LIMITED
The Old Candlemakers, West Street, Lewes, East Sussex BN7 2NZ

*Creative Director:* PETER BRIDGEWATER
*Art Director:* CLARE BARBER
*Designer:* JANE LANAWAY
*DTP Designer:* CHRIS LANAWAY
*Editorial Director:* SOPHIE COLLINS
*Managing Editor:* ANNE TOWNLEY
*Senior Project Editor:* ROWAN DAVIES
*Editor:* MANDY GREENFIELD
*Studio Photography:* LIZ EDDISON, GUY RYECART
*Illustrations:* MADELEINE HARDIE
*Models:* MARK JAMIESON
*Picture Researcher:* LIZ EDDISON

Originated and printed by Hong Kong Graphics and Printing Ltd

This book is typeset in Bembo and Gill

Page 2 illustration: The dramatic Oriental poppy
Cover illustrations: Clive Nichols

## PICTURE CREDITS

# contents

# introduction
# the pleasures of color

*By matching the color of flower and foliage, a particular mood can be created. Here, the brilliant red of Crocosmia 'Lucifer' is echoed by the foliage of Prunus × cistena.*

Welcome to the wonderful world of color, or more specifically the world of color in the garden. The golden glow of yellow, the vibrancy of shocking pink, the dynamism of bright red, the softness of grass green, and the tranquility of deep blue—all are there among flower, fruit, and foliage color for you to discover, use, and enjoy in your garden. There are literally thousands of different hues to be found among plants, giving us innumerable opportunities to create beautiful color combinations.

The problem is that the average gardener, faced with the choice of myriad plants at the garden center, is so busy checking whether a plant will grow in his or her particular soil and worrying about whether there is enough sunlight that all thought of whether it will fit into the current color scheme is forgotten. So yet another plant is purchased to join the mixture of colors in the border.

All is not lost, however. Whether you want a quiet green oasis in which to relax after a hard day's work; the excitement of a mass of rainbow colors in your back yard; or whether you hanker after the quintessential English mixture of soft pinks, grays, and lavender so beloved of that great gardener Gertrude Jekyll—all are within the abilities of even the novice gardener, simply by following a few basic rules.

*A blue border can offer a tranquil feel to an area of a garden.* Aconitum *'Spark's Variety', blue delphiniums, and* Viola cornuta *have all been successfully planted together here.*

LOBELIA 'CAMBRIDGE BLUE'

This book sets out those rules and shows how you can put plants together to make attractive and exciting color schemes. It has been carefully designed to be compact enough to carry around the garden or nursery, and it is tough enough to put up with constant handling as you seek the right plant for each particular bed and border.

The first part of the book explains how color harmonies work and how you can adapt them to help you put plants together in your beds and borders. If you have ever tried planning color schemes in your house, or given thought to the colors of the clothes you wear, then you will find it simple to plan for color in your garden, whether it is a small back yard in the middle of a city or a larger garden set in the countryside.

It really is worthwhile reading through Part One before starting to plan your garden; you will then be able to decide which color schemes you would like to try out in the different areas of it.

Part Two is the color directory, with tabbed pages to take you straight to the color you need. There are seven separate color sections, starting with yellow, then working through orange to red, pink, purple, and blue, ending with white. Each tabbed section gives you information about the specific color, which other hues can be used

with the color in question, and how to use it to the best effect in your garden. In each section flower colors come first, followed by fruit and then foliage color.

*The yellow flowers of this Euphorbia sikkimensis positively glow among the green foliage.*

Green has not been included as a separate tabbed section, as almost all plants have green leaves and we could have filled the whole book with different shades of green. Ideas for using green as a color are given in Part One, and in the tabbed sections in Part Two advice is given on using green with each of the other colors in your garden.

*Plants in containers, such as this standard marguerite, can add an extra dimension to gardens.*

There are many leaves that are colored other than green, and these are included in the appropriate tabbed sections—so purple and plum foliage is to be found in the purple section; yellow foliage and yellow-variegated leaves in the yellow section; and gray and silver foliage in the white.

This book was written with the intention of making color planning in your garden as simple, enjoyable, and effective as possible. We enjoyed preparing and writing the book and we hope you get the same pleasure out of reading and using it.

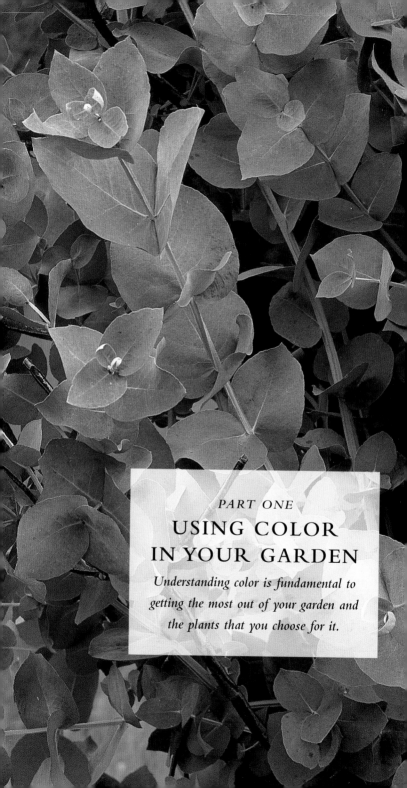

PART ONE

# USING COLOR
# IN YOUR GARDEN

*Understanding color is fundamental to
getting the most out of your garden and
the plants that you choose for it.*

# the nature of color
## colors of the spectrum

To understand the various ways in which colors can be used, and how different colors influence each other, it is helpful to look at the spectrum, or color wheel.

### THE SPECTRUM

The spectrum is the range of colors produced when light passes through a prism. It is usually displayed as a wheel in which the colors of the rainbow form a circle. Rainbows are created when sunlight passes through rain, which acts as a prism, splitting sunlight into the well-known color order of red, orange, yellow, green, blue, indigo, and violet. These same colors, known as hues, are found in the spectrum. One point to note is that all the colors included in the spectrum are pure colors. This means that they contain no white or black.

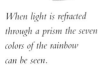

*When light is refracted through a prism the seven colors of the rainbow can be seen.*

*The secondary colors— orange, green, and purple —appear between their parent primary colors in the spectrum.*

### PRIMARY AND SECONDARY COLORS

The spectrum consists of three primary colors: red, yellow, and blue. These colors are called primary because they are distinct from each other and contain no pigment of any other color. All the other colors are created by mixing different proportions of the primary colors together and by adding white, gray, or black to the mixture. A mix of equal proportions of two of the primary colors gives the three

secondary colors: orange, a mixture of equal parts of red and yellow; green, a mixture of equal parts of yellow and blue; and purple, a mixture of equal parts of red and blue. If you ever tried mixing paints at school, then you will know that a mixture of all three primary colors results in a very dark brown or near black. In the spectrum the six primary and secondary colors are arranged so that the three primary colors are spaced equidistantly around the circle, with each secondary color spaced in between two parent primary colors. So the order is red, orange, yellow, green, blue, purple, and then red again.

### INTERMEDIATE COLORS

A simple spectrum includes just the primary and secondary colors, but it is rather more interesting when some intermediate colors are also shown. These are arranged between the primary and secondary colors and contain varying proportions of two of the primary colors.

*Blue is an easy color to use in the garden as it harmonizes well with the surrounding foliage.*

*Intermediate colors are placed between the primary and secondary colors to create a wider spectrum.*

# the nature of color
## tints, tones, and shades

*The dazzling white of these hyacinths shows how pure their color is. Many other flowers have just a hint of white in them, while the soft pastel flowers include a large amount of white.*

To create the full range of colors found in nature, black, gray, and white can be added to the spectral hues. Colors formed by adding white are called tints; those formed by adding gray are called tones; and those formed by adding black, shades. Tints, tones, and shades vary in depth depending on the proportion of hue to white, gray, and black. When all the tints, tones, and shades of all the primary, secondary, and intermediate colors are put together, we have a palette of well over a thousand discernibly different colors from which to choose.

### TINTS

The proportion of white to color varies from just a drop of white to almost all white. The smallest proportion of white to color gives us deep pastel colors, such as sunflower-yellow, apricot, deep pink, sky blue, and lilac, whereas adding more white produces paler colors, like primrose, pale apricot, rose-pink, light blue, and lavender. Add more white to color, and soft tints of pale yellow, buff, pale pink, and pale blue are created; adding still more white produces the creams and off-whites that contain just a suggestion of another color. There are a multitude of different tints found in flowers because the pale colors—particularly the pale shades of blue and yellow—attract numerous insects for pollination and so are abundant in nature.

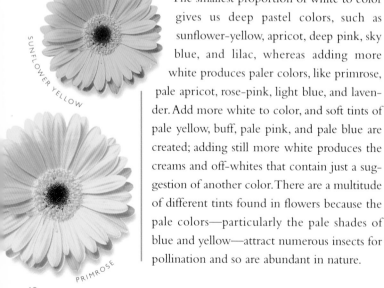

SUNFLOWER YELLOW

PRIMROSE

RED

DUSKY ROSE

ORANGE

BROWN

### TONES

Gray plus color creates tones in which the hue is still discernible, although it is subdued and darkened. Yellow changes to yellow ocher, orange to terra cotta and sienna, red to dusky rose, and blue to deep blue and indigo. There are a few plants whose flowers are tones—they include the euphorbias and some of the old-fashioned roses—and these are always interesting to use in color schemes. Stem colors are often tones of orange, while leaves come in a variety of tones of green, including the gray-green leaves of daffodils and many of the conifers.

### SHADES

When mixed with hues, black gives us shades; but unlike tones, which merely darken, adding black to create shades often changes the basic hue completely. Orange turns to brown when black is added, red to carmine, and blue to navy. A small amount of black with green gives us the color of many of our deciduous tree leaves, such as oak and beech; add more black and we have the color of pine needles. There are a few dark flowers, usually shades of purple (as in *Delphinium* 'Black Knight'), but there is also a range of deep red flowers (as in *Melianthus major*). These deep-colored flowers are extremely valuable, as they can be used to give extra impact to our planting schemes. The shades most frequently seen in gardens are those of orange, which when mixed with black creates brown—the color of the stems and trunks of the majority of woody plants.

# the nature of color
# color harmonies

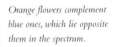

Having identified hundreds of different colors, we now need to know how to combine them successfully. Artists through the ages have studied colors and their interaction with one another and have put forward various theories and rules concerning color harmonies. These include "the harmony of tints, tones, and shades" using a single color, and "the harmony of adjacent colors," as well as "the harmony of opposite colors" (which are also called complementary colors) when using two colors.

*Orange flowers complement blue ones, which lie opposite them in the spectrum.*

### SINGLE-COLOR HARMONIES

The first theory of color harmony is that the tints, tones, and shades of any one hue harmonize: so pinks, reds, dusky roses, and deep plums look very attractive planted together, just

*This beautiful array shows how well different tints, tones, and shades of red work when planted together.*

as appealing combinations can also be achieved by mixing golds, primroses, and the lemon-yellows; or try using orange, apricot, and buff together for an effective display. Frequently in the countryside you can see a natural harmony of the tints, tones, and shades of green in all its variety, and this is perhaps the very simplest harmony to try out in the garden.

## ADJACENT COLOR HARMONIES

The second theory states that any two colors that are situated adjacent to each other in the spectrum form a natural color harmony. Such harmonies are readily found in nature—we see a harmony of red and orange in fall leaves, and a combination of reds and mauves in the sky at sunset. These color harmonies are deeply satisfying, particularly when the two colors are seen as large expanses of a single color. In the garden the color green is almost always present, providing half of any color combination. Its adjacent colors are yellow and blue—so daffodils planted amid grass or bluebells in woodland look terrific. To use other adjacent color harmonies, it is necessary to reduce the amount of green, by using gray or other colored foliage.

## OPPOSITE AND COMPLEMENTARY HARMONIES

The third theory states that any two colors that lie directly opposite each other in the spectral circle will harmonize. These include yellow as opposite and complementary to purple, red to green, and orange to blue. Every color in the spectrum (plus all the various tints, tones, and shades) has an opposite and complementary color. In the garden it is sufficient to interpret and use the three primary colors and their secondary color opposites in order to create a stunning effect.

*Planting complementary colors together, such as purple and yellow, will create a natural harmony. Here yellow tulips have been placed among blue hyacinths and purple pansies.*

## color in the garden
# background color

*It is important to consider any existing features in a garden, in order to plant sensitively around them.*

No garden, whether existing or projected, is entirely without some color before new planting starts: there will always be a groundscape—perhaps gray paving, brown earth, or green grass; and possibly some containment—dark green hedges, red brick walls, brown fences, or a screen of green trees. There may also be the color of nearby houses or countryside to consider. Depending on the part of the world in which you live, the background will vary from the dark green of conifers in far northern countries to the lush, rich greens of tropical areas.

### PARKLAND GREENS

In temperate areas, including Britain, the natural vegetation is deciduous woodland with grass as ground cover—this gives a background of assorted greens, which can vary from the fresh lime-green of young leaves in spring to the dark, almost black green, of yew trees. Against this background the colors blue and yellow (which are adjacent to green in the spectrum) are attractive to use in planting, mirroring the colors of nature in springtime. At the other extreme, red (which is opposite and complementary to green) causes drama and excitement.

*The natural landscape of Britain is abundant with lush greens, as seen in this wood.*

## MEDITERRANEAN HEAT

In warmer and drier parts of the world, such as the Mediterranean, there is often insufficient rainfall for grass to be able to survive, and trees and shrubs are less vigorous, so the background color changes to muted, neutral colors of sandy soil, olive-green foliage, and light brown hills. Green is often absent from these areas, so almost any color scheme can be used, including very bright colors. Think of street plantings where the shocking pink of bougainvillea is mixed with the bright red of hibiscus and the clear blue of plumbago or jacaranda, adding color to the backdrop of white houses and dusty roads.

*Shocking pink bougainvillea is typical of the vibrant plant colors found in the Mediterranean.*

In cooler and wetter parts of the world, the same neutral background colors can often be found in enclosed town gardens, where bright colors can similarly be used to bring dull gray paving and walls to vibrant life.

## TROPICAL GREENS

In tropical areas the leaves are larger in size and of a much brighter green, and many of the bright red or yellow native flowers look wonderful against the intense blue of the sky. Copy this rainbow effect or, for a more relaxing planting, use plenty of white or pastel-colored flowers, with green-and-white variegated foliage. In temperate gardens, conservatories can create an oasis of bright color amid the muted greens and soft yellows of the garden.

*PALM LEAVES*

# color in the garden
# the effect of sunlight

One of the considerations when using color in our gardens, as opposed to in our homes, is the effect sunlight has on plants as it rises, shines, and sets during the day and as it changes with the seasons. Light intensity can range from the dim light of a foggy winter's dawn to the glare of full sunlight at noon on a hot summer's day. In indoor terms this could be likened to a single 25-watt ceiling bulb being replaced with several 1000-watt spotlights.

## FULL SUNLIGHT

Strong light bleaches colors, as anyone who has been to a tropical beach will know; the colorful shirt bought in the Caribbean looks positively garish when worn in more temperate regions. Beds and borders placed in full sunlight can contain the gaudiest of flowers and they will look bright and cheerful all summer. But, if planted with flowers of pastel tints (like many of the azaleas), the soft colors will be bleached as soon as the sun shines and will lose their impact, looking pale and grubby. Lovely English borders of pale pink, blue, and lavender glow on a dull day in northern climes, but they look completely "washed-out" under a blazing summer sun.

*Areas that receive direct sunlight should be planted with brightly colored flowers. Any paler flowers will look completely bleached when the sun hits them.*

## SOFT SUNLIGHT AND PARTIAL SHADE

Dappled shade at the edge of woodlands, or the light of early morning and evening, allows the paler colors to glow. Many evening flowers fall into this color range, including evening primrose in pale yellow and tobacco plants in tints of pink and green. In this light, colors appear clear and true to tone and the blues really come into their own. In full sunlight blue fades to almost white, and in full shade it disappears into the shadows, but in a gentle sun it becomes distinguishable from nearby greens and can really be appreciated.

*Pale colors really glow in evening sunlight. The gentle sun on these plants has served to bring out their colors.*

## OVERCAST CONDITIONS AND FULL SHADE

Woodlands can be dark places, at least in the summer, with the same light intensity as overcast days in the winter. In low light, white positively glows and yellow adds light and warmth. Shiny leaves reflect the light and can be effective in relieving the gloom. Avoid blue and purple, which tend to disappear into the shadows, as does red; however, the paler tints of these three colors can start to lighten the darkness. Orange can also work well in this light if the dark pastels (such as apricot) or the paler buff colors are used.

*Foliage works well in overcast conditions, as it picks up and reflects whatever light there is. Adding pale tints among the green can also lift a shaded area.*

# color in the garden
## seasonal changes

Light levels change on a daily and seasonal basis, as do the backgrounds of the planting schemes in our gardens as the dead branches of winter slowly give way to the unfurling lime-green leaves of spring, and then progress to the full richness of the summer greens. These in turn gradually change to the browns, reds, oranges, and yellows of fall leaves, which finally drop and everything becomes dormant again.

*JASMINUM OFFICINALE 'FIONA SUNRISE'*

### WINTER

Winter is typified by short days, low temperatures, and a sun that barely gets above the horizon before it seems to slink away again. Low light levels make the very palest flowers glow against the pale blue sky, and every bit of color is welcome in the garden to compensate for the dark green of dormant lawns and the dark brown—almost black—of the trunks and stems of deciduous trees and shrubs.

In less temperate areas winter is a time for a monochromatic landscape of the black branches of trees and shrubs outlined against the crisp whiteness of snow. Strong color schemes can be extremely successful and one of the most cheerful combinations for the winter garden is the bright red stems of the dogwoods in combination with the blue-green foliage of junipers viewed against a background of white birch stems.

*In the winter the very palest color schemes glow against the dark greens of the surrounding trees and shrubs.*

*These bluebells and stitchwort typify the fresh vibrancy of spring colors emerging through the grass.*

*The richness of the greens during summer is complemented well by these red flowers.*

*The warm, mellow light of fall enhances the russets and yellows that are found in the plants at this time of year.*

## SPRING

In spring nature bursts forth and new leaves of lime-green start to emerge; the grass appears greener as it starts into fresh growth and early flowers appear. Many of these flowers are yellow (daffodils, primroses) and pale-pink (cherry blossom). There are also blues and whites (scillas, hawthorn), but all the colors are soft. Follow nature's lead and put pink and white hellebores under almond trees, or lots of daffodils with forsythia.

## SUMMER

During summer, the grass is a rich green, while all the trees are in full leaf in a myriad of greens, from the yellow-greens of the Indian bean tree, to the bright green of ash and birch and the darker shades of oak and beech. Bright colors come into their own now, and reds look particularly attractive—either in a rose garden or in a red border. To avoid green, try using all-gray foliage and then add shocking pinks and purples; or use yellow foliage, then add yellow and purple flowers.

## FALL

The season of mists and mellow fruitfulness means warm yellow light and all the gentle russet colors of fall foliage and fruit—everywhere there is a golden glow, which brings fall borders to life. Try a color scheme in your garden of yellows and oranges using chrysanthemums and heleniums or, for a rather more subtle scheme, use the blues and mauves of New York daisies together with the pale pinks of Japanese anemones.

# color in the garden
## color schemes

*Magazine features, such as this one showing* Potentilla *'Gibson's Scarlet', can provide inspiration for your borders.*

Now it is time to start planning your beds and borders and putting the theory into practice. First, select your color scheme, using either hues that you love and that make you feel happy or a scheme that complements the color of your house or the existing features in your garden. Second, decide on the type of plants you want to grow in your garden—perhaps all herbaceous plants, as in the traditional herbaceous border; a rose bed with an edging of lavender; an all-shrub border, or possibly a mixture of roses, shrubs, and herbaceous plants.

Next, look up the entries for your chosen color in the plant directory in Part Two and make a list of the plants that you would like to use. As you do so, make a note of the heights of the different plants, because you will need lower plants at the front of your border and taller plants at the back.

Check the growing requirements of the individual plants. Do they need full sun or shade? Are they happy in wet or dry conditions? Are they fussy about the type of soil? All the plants you select should need the same conditions and should suit the soil, aspect, and drainage that are found in the proposed part of your garden.

Opposite and overleaf are some suggested plant lists to try out for different color schemes and varying growing conditions in your garden.

## A YELLOW AND PURPLE MIXED BORDER IN FULL SUN

Plants that have either deep yellow or rich emperor-purple flowers would brighten up any garden, but they look at their most effective when planted in front of a gray stone wall. Try planting the smaller plants in groups of three or five of the same type together, then repeat your favorite plants along the border.

*These yellow lupines and purple allium look magnificent planted against a wall covered with trellis.*

*The nodding flowers of Clematis orientalis, a vigorous climber which will thrive scrambling up a wall or trellis.*

### SUGGESTED PLANTS

| | |
|---|---|
| ON BACK WALL | *Clematis orientalis* |
| | *Fremontodendron californicum* |
| | *Solanum crispum* 'Glasnevin' |
| | *Vitis vinifera* 'Purpurea' |
| BACK OF BORDER | *Achillea filipendulina* 'Gold Plate' |
| | *Aster × frikartii* 'Mönch' |
| | *Buddleja davidii* 'Black Knight' |
| | *Delphinium* 'Black Knight' |
| | *Physocarpus opulifolius* 'Luteus' |
| MIDDLE / FRONT OF BORDER | *Campanula glomerata* 'Superba' |
| | *Coreopsis verticillata* 'Moonbeam' |
| | *Erigeron* 'Darkest of All' |
| | *Oenothera fruticosa* |
| | *Potentilla* 'Yellow Queen' |
| | *Salvia × sylvestris* 'May Night' |
| | *Veronica spicata* 'Romiley Purple' |

*EUONYMUS
FORTUNEI
'SILVER
QUEEN'*

## A GREEN AND WHITE PLANTING FOR A SHADY CORNER

This planting needs to offer interest and color all year round, to ensure plants have been selected so that at least one plant is in flower every month. The narcissus adds extra spring color and the impatiens injects color in the summer months. A white winter-flowering pansy is included in the list—this will not be found in the white tabbed section, but a similar pansy can be found under purple annuals (see p. 138).

These plants would grow equally well if planted in tubs, grouped together in a shady basement or courtyard. Or you could group them around a pale gray stone statue or perhaps beside a white-painted summerhouse.

### SUGGESTED PLANTS

| | |
|---|---|
| SPRING | *Dicentra spectabilis* 'Alba'<br>*Narcissus* 'Mount Hood' |
| SUMMER | *Impatiens* 'Accent White'<br>*Nicotiana* 'Domino White' |
| FALL | *Anemone × hybrida* 'Honorine Jobert'<br>*Cimicifuga simplex* 'White Pearl' |
| WINTER | *Helleborus niger*<br>*Viola* 'Universal White' |
| ALL YEAR ROUND | *Euonymus fortunei* 'Silver Queen'<br>*Hedera helix* 'Glacier' |

*The intensity of* Crocosmia *'Lucifer' helps to create a "hot" scheme in this bed during the late summer and fall months.*

## A "HOT" COLOR SCHEME FOR THE FALL

This is a planting scheme to provide both flower and foliage color in the late summer and fall. Most of the plants prefer full sun but will tolerate some shade for part of the day. A touch of blue is added for extra interest. To extend the season use some of the orange annuals, like *Zinnia elegans* 'Short Stuff Orange'.

*PHYGELIUS × RECTUS 'AFRICAN QUEEN'*

## GREEN AND YELLOW PLANTING FOR A DAMP AREA

There are often damp areas in a garden, which may be due to a variety of reasons, including an underlying clay soil or impeded drainage. Alternatively, you may be lucky enough to have a stream running through your garden with damp margins on either side of it. All the suggested plants, with yellow flowers or foliage, enjoy moist or even wet soils.

*Damp areas are perfect for creating a striking effect with foliage, such as that of* Pleioblastus auricomus.

Among the annual plants there are one or two that prefer a damp soil, including mimulus, which—although it is listed with the orange flowers—has several yellow-flowering cultivars that could be added for extra summer color.

# color in the garden
# flower color

*Poppies can often appear slightly paler than their true color; this is due to the translucent nature of their petals.*

There is a wonderful range of flower colors to use, with every hue of the spectrum available, although the range of greens is rather limited. There is also a full range of tints of the various hues, but rather a restricted range in the tones and shades. Our perception of a plant's color varies with the texture of the petals: the translucent glow of the papery petals of poppies makes them appear paler, while the velvety richness of petunia petals gives them greater depth of color. Choose according to the color as it appears to you when you look at the plant and not according to the catalog description!

Your type of soil can affect flower color: many hydrangeas have flowers that are pink when the soil is alkaline but bright blue when it is acid. Other plants show more subtle changes—a salmon-colored rose in one garden will appear pinky rose in another.

## ADDING EXTRA
## IMPACT WITH ANNUALS

*Annuals, such as this marigold, will give instant color to a bed or border.*

If you crave great splashes of color, then look no farther than the annuals, for these plants have a greater ratio of flowers to leaf than any of the other plants, and many of them flower all summer. One note of caution: although many, like marigolds and petunias, are naturally bright-colored, various popular annuals have been

cross-bred over the years to produce bigger, better, and more exciting flowers. The result is that some are now so strongly colored that they appear positively garish, particularly when planted next to each other. Annuals also need to be planted each year, which can be costly, unless you are prepared to grow them from seed. But they really are indispensable for adding extra impact to your color scheme.

*When planning beds it is important to ensure that some of the plants are long-flowering, so that the effect of the chosen color scheme lasts for as long as possible.*

## LONG-SEASON FLOWERS

Some of the most dramatic flowers (lupines, irises, peonies) appear for a relatively short time and any color scheme based on them will have only a brief moment of glory. However, if your other plants have longer flowering seasons, they can continue the effect of the color scheme. Add penstemons, daylilies, scabious, and catmint (all of which flower for most of the summer) and, best of all, shrub roses, such as *Rosa* 'Felicia'. For late-summer borders use echinaceas and fuchsias, which carry flowers until the first frosts.

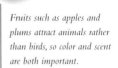

# color in the garden
# fruit color

After flowering, all plants produce seeds in some form of fruiting body, and in many cases these can be as colorful as the flowers. Fruits are designed as a means of ensuring that the seeds of plants are dispersed, birds often being the chosen means of dispersal—they eat the berries, but the seeds pass harmlessly through their gut to be eliminated, and they can then germinate in a suitable situation.

Birds are attracted by the hot colors of red, scarlet, and orange, so many berries are found in this coloration. Larger fruits, like apples and pears, are designed to be eaten by animals and, although color may be important, other factors such as scent may also be an inducement. Fruits are normally produced in the late summer and fall, when they also brighten up our gardens, particularly those in the red and orange color range.

*Fruits such as apples and plums attract animals rather than birds, so color and scent are both important.*

*The vibrant color of this* Pyracantha *will brighten up any garden and attract birds to it.*

## DARK PLUM AND BLACK FRUITS

There are many fruits which, when ripe, are dark red, plum, or almost black in color. Where the fruits have a shiny skin, as in elderberries, these dark colors become more noticeable and could be included in any scheme that includes plum or mauve.

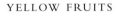

RIPE BLACKBERRY FRUITS

## YELLOW FRUITS

Birds avoid yellow fruits and leave them hanging on the tree, which is to our advantage, giving us extra color into the winter. We have diligent plant collectors and breeders to thank for creating the delights of the yellow-berried *Pyracantha* 'Soleil d'Or' and *Viburnum opulus* 'Xanthocarpum'.

YELLOW BERRIES OF *ILEX AQUIFOLIUM* 'BACCIFLAVA'.

## WHITE FRUITS

There are a few plants producing white berries, including the white pearly berries of *Symphoricarpos × doorenbosii* 'White Hedge' and *Gaultheria mucronata* 'White Pearl'. Mistle thrushes eat mistletoe, so perhaps they happen to prefer white to red. There are really not enough white berries to make a separate entry in the plant directory, but look out for them at the nursery and garden center.

THE WHITE BERRIES OF *SORBUS KOEHNEANA*.

## BLUE FRUITS

Blue fruits look almost out of place, as though invisible painters have been out overnight painting our red berries blue. Their color can be almost turquoise and, seen against a backdrop of fall leaves, they give a wonderful example of orange and blue working as complementary colors.

THE STRIKING BLUE OF *VIBURNUM DAVIDII* FRUIT.

# color in the garden
## foliage and stems

Many gardeners think of color in their garden in terms only of flower color and they completely ignore foliage, to the extent that they will state quite categorically that their garden has no color in it when the flowers are over. How wrong they are—there is color present in any garden at any time of year, even in winter, in the variety of greens found in evergreen leaves. In spring, summer, and fall there is an enormous variety of foliage color, with a palette of different greens.

HEDERA HELIX

### EVERGREEN LEAVES

Evergreen plants, whether shrubs or herbaceous perennials, are immensely valuable because they provide year-round interest. Most evergreens have green foliage, but there are a few colored-leaved plants in this group, including the yellow-leaved heather *Calluna vulgaris* 'Gold Haze', the plum-colored *Phormium tenax* 'Purpureum', and the green-and-white variegated *Euonymus fortunei* 'Silver Queen'. Surprisingly, many of the gray-leaved plants retain their leaves in winter and should perhaps be labeled "evergray!" It is important to note that with the low light of winter some plants that have colored leaves in summer become completely green in winter— examples are the golden marjoram *Origanum vulgare* 'Aureum' and *Lonicera nitida* 'Baggesen's Gold'.

*Hollies, such as* Ilex aquifolium *'Wateriana', have variegated foliage that will give added interest in the months when a garden is not in flower.*

COLOR IN THE GARDEN

## GRAY FOLIAGE

There is a whole range of plants with gray leaves, most of which like to grow in dry, sunny parts of the garden. The gray is a useful foil for brightly colored flowers; for instance, *Cistus × pulverulentus* 'Sunset', which has shocking pink flowers, or *Phlomis fruti-*

*cosa*, with bright yellow blooms. Other gray-foliage plants have soft lilac-blue flowers, as is seen in many of the herbs, including rosemary, sage, and lavender.

*Plants with gray or silver foliage work well when planted with bright flowers, such as these red nasturtiums and geraniums.*

## YELLOW FOLIAGE

Some plants have all-yellow foliage; others have yellow-and-green variegated foliage, where only part of the leaf is yellow and the rest green. Both types of foliage are useful as part of a yellow color scheme. Add other green-leaved plants with yellow flowers for a yellow-green adjacent harmony, or some purple flowers to make a stunning combination of complementary colors.

*HEUCHERA MICRANTHA*
*'PALACE PURPLE'*

## PLUM OR PURPLE FOLIAGE

We use the terms copper, plum, or purple foliage, but plants with these leaves are visually so similar that they belong in a single category. Use them as part of your color schemes; as a deep red in red-green harmonies; as purple, with mauves or blues, in adjacent color plantings; or contrast them with yellows—all of these will look good in your garden.

## GLAUCOUS FOLIAGE

In some leaves there is a definite blue haze to the underlying green and this foliage is called glaucous or blue (it is really a light blue-green). This is a wonderful colored foliage to use: mix it with plum foliage and green-and-white variegated leaves; or go for the startling impact of deep pink flowers against glaucous foliage.

*The glaucous leaves of Hosta sieboldiana var. elegans look great when planted among other types of foliage.*

## FALL COLOR

Some plants, whose leaves appear a rather ordinary green, suddenly change at the onset of fall into a Jacob's coat of scarlet and orange. Notice how a Virginia creeper bursts into a firework display as the flowers around it fade. Although many of the fall-foliage plants prefer acid soil, every garden deserves at least one area devoted to these plants.

## STEM AND BARK COLOR

The usual color of stems is green for herbaceous plants and brown for woody plants, but some break this norm by having red, yellow, white, or even stripy stems. The best group of garden plants for stem color is the dogwood, including *Cornus alba* and *Cornus stolonifera* 'Flaviramea'. White stems can be found most obviously in the birches, but are also present in several species of *Rubus*.

32

# PART TWO

# THE PLANT DIRECTORY

*The symbols shown here are used throughout the plant directory. They give an indication of each plant's main characteristics and growing requirements, but for full details you should consult the written description of each plant.*

| | | | |
|---|---|---|---|
| SHADE | | ACID SOIL |
| PARTIAL SHADE | | 20°F (-6°C) AND BELOW |
| LIGHT SHADE | | |
| FULL SUN | | SLIGHT FROST/ DOWN TO 20°F (-6°C) |
| FULL SUN OR LIGHT/PARTIAL SHADE | | NOT BELOW 32°F (0°C) |
| WELL-DRAINED SOIL | | SCENTED FLOWERS |
| WELL-DRAINED BUT MOISTURE-RETENTIVE SOIL | | UNSCENTED FLOWERS |
| WET SOIL | | EASY TO GROW |
| NEUTRAL SOIL | | MODERATELY EASY TO GROW |
| ALKALINE SOIL | | |

# how to use
# the tabbed sections

ROSA 'NEW DAWN'

The following seven tabbed sections have been designed to make mixing and matching colors in your garden as easy and foolproof as possible. Yellow comes first, followed by orange, red, pink, purple, blue, and finally white. White does not actually feature in the color spectrum, but it features heavily when planning a garden. Pink is usually considered just a tint of red, but there are so many pink flowers that we made an exception.

Each tabbed section starts with a few notes on using a specific color in the garden, then lists selected plants. In each section flowers come first, followed by fruit and then foliage. Within the flower pages, annuals and biennials feature first, followed by bulbs, herbaceous perennials, shrubs, and climbers. We decided not to include trees and conifers, as color is not usually a major factor in their selection.

We could include only a limited number of plants, so if a particular plant is listed in one color or category, then it will not usually appear elsewhere. For instance, there are many different-colored daylilies (*Hemerocallis*), but the only entry is under yellow (*see p.47*). However, where there is a range of other colors this is

YELLOW

🌥 🗯 🔲 🌧 ✿ ⚇

RUDBECKIA FULGIDA  ⎤       ——— BOTANICAL
    'GOLDSTURM'                  NAME
RUDBECKIA SPECIOSA  ⎤
    'GOLDSTURM'                ——— EARLIER
    CONEFLOWER             BOTANICAL
  *Herbaceous perennial*       NAME

A bushy and clump-forming plant,      ——— COMMON
with oblong to lance-shaped green      NAME
leaves and large yellow flowers, up
to 13cm (5in) wide and with dark
brown, cone-like centres, from    ——— TYPE OF
mid-summer to early autumn.      PLANT
  Lift and divide congested plants
every three or four years; replant
young pieces from around the
outside of the clump.

mentioned, and an index at the end of each section includes plants in other sections that also have varieties of that color.

## ANNUALS AND BIENNIALS

There are thousands of different annuals and biennials and we have tried to include a representative selection. Annuals in particular are a useful way to try out a proposed color scheme: find three or four in the appropriate tabbed sections, plant up a container or small bed with your choice and watch the colors emerge. If it is unsatisfactory, then at the end of the summer you can remove the plants and try again; if it looks great, choose the same colors from within the herbaceous perennial, shrub, and climber pages and plan a permanent planting, following the guidelines given in the section on color schemes. Don't worry if you cannot find the exact variety of annual listed in the directory—just find one of the same color.

## BULBS

Bulbs also come in hundreds of different named varieties. Tulips alone come in virtually every color possible. Bulbs can be used for trial color schemes—they are usually planted in the fall, with spring bedding plants like wallflowers; in the spring you can see the effect of your choice. Remember that sunlight and seasons affect the way in which colors appear, so a scheme using annuals that does not work in the summer may still be attractive using tulips and wallflowers in the spring.

*Tulips come in a wide assortment of colors, so they are useful for trying out different color schemes during the spring months.*

## HERBACEOUS PLANTS

These give the main flower color to our mixed borders and need to be chosen for their position in the border, as well as for color: low-growing plants for the front and taller ones for the back.

## SHRUBS

The shrubs listed under flower color were selected for having masses of flowers in season. Despite being smothered in blooms and there being thousands of cultivars available, there was room for at most one rhododendron and one rose in each shrub section (unfortunately there are no true blue roses for the blue section). Study the details of the rhododendrons and roses included in this book, then look at the range available in your local nursery. In the foliage section there is a selection of shrubs that are more important for their colored foliage than for either the color or splendour of their flowers.

## CLIMBERS

Climbers need very careful selection, as they form a backdrop to our color schemes. Choose them either for colored flowers that will form part of the overall color scheme of your border, or for green or colored foliage as a background or foil to the flowers that are positioned in front.

*Giving thought to where plants will be positioned in a border will ensure that there is color throughout.*

*LONICERA ×
BROWNII
'DROPMORE
SCARLET'*

# YELLOW

*Yellow brings a touch of sunshine to the gloomiest of days and is found in profusion in nature.*

# the color yellow
# yellow plants

*HELIANTHUS ANNUUS*

A wide palette of yellow colors is found in plants, mostly in flowers but also in foliage and in fruit (as in the pale yellow fruits of *Sorbus* 'Joseph Rock'), and even in the color of their stems (as in *Salix alba* 'Vitellina'). Yellow flower colors range from the creamy flowers of *Stachyurus praecox*, through the pale yellow of primroses in spring to the lemon-yellow of *Trollius europaeus* and the golden-yellow of *Helianthus* 'Loddon Gold'.

In foliage the color range is mostly in the middle part of the spectrum, but ranges from the yellowy green leaves of *Hosta* 'Sun Power' through the greeny yellow leaves of *Origanum vulgare* 'Aureum' to the bright golden-yellow that is found in the leaves of *Philadelphus coronarius* 'Aureus'.

### COLOR HARMONIES

Yellow is an easy color to use in the garden as, being adjacent to green in the spectrum, it forms a natural harmony with the surrounding foliage. For a brighter effect use yellow foliage with yellow flowers, creating interest by including all the various tints, tones, and shades of yellow, from palest primrose to dark olive. In summer and fall combine the brighter yellows with orange and scarlet to produce a sizzling-hot scheme. The contrast-color to yellow is purple and, for a dramatic

*All the various shades of yellow work well in the garden; the golden color of this* Rudbeckia *adds warmth during the fall.*

border, combine bright yellow and deep purple flowers, with yellow foliage to complete the picture. A softer scheme uses pale yellow and lavender flowers with gray foliage.

*Yellow foliage and flowers, such as those found in* Lysimachia punctata, Gaillardia *'Goblin', fennel, and* Hemerocallis *'Bonanza', will brighten up any bed or border.*

## USING YELLOW IN YOUR GARDEN

Yellow brightens up the dullest of garden areas. Use yellow foliage and flowers wherever their brightness will give maximum pleasure—for instance, yellow-variegated hostas and yellow privet in a shady town garden; or mahonias and winter jasmine by the front door in the middle of winter. Yellow is seen naturally in spring in wild daffodils and primroses—so bring this effect into your garden with cultivated varieties; for greater effect, add yellow crocuses and tulips. Blue or purple also accompanies yellow in nature—for example, violets with primroses, and blue speedwell with daffodils. Fall is another season for using yellow; try yellow and orange dahlias and chrysanthemums in front of fall-coloring foliage.

## CALCEOLARIA INTEGRIFOLIA
### 'SUNSHINE'
**CALCEOLARIA RUGOSA 'SUNSHINE'**
BUSH CALCEOLARIA
*Semihardy annual*

A strongly colored, bushy, and slightly sprawling tender perennial, usually raised as a semihardy annual for introducing vivid color to hanging-baskets and window boxes, as well as in summer-bedding displays in borders. From midsummer to early fall it reveals bright yellow, pouchlike flowers.

☀ HEIGHT 8–10in (20–25cm)

☀ SPREAD 10–12in (25–30cm)

☀ SITUATION Full sun or partial shade

☀ SOIL Light, and moisture-retentive but well-drained

☀ HARDINESS Will not tolerate temperatures below 32°F (0°C)

☀ ZONES 4–8 as annual

## HELIANTHUS ANNUUS
### 'TEDDY BEAR'
SUNFLOWER
*Hardy annual*

A superb dwarf sunflower with 6in (15cm) wide, golden-yellow, extra-double flowers from midsummer to early fall. This variety is ideal for filling borders with color.

Other varieties extend the color range to several shades of yellow, as well as velvety red, deep crimson, and cream.

☀ HEIGHT 1½–2ft (45–60cm)

☀ SPREAD 1¼–1½ ft (38–45cm)

☀ SITUATION Full sun and shelter from wind

☀ SOIL Light and well-drained

☀ HARDINESS Tolerates slight frost

☀ ZONES Warm-season annual in zones 2–11

**LIMNANTHES DOUGLASII**
MEADOW-FOAM
*Hardy annual*

A low and soil-smothering annual with glossy, pale-green, and deeply cut leaves. Fragrant, funnel-shaped, white flowers with dominant yellow centers appear from early to late summer.

This is an ideal annual for edging borders and paths, as well as for adding color to newly constructed rock gardens.

☀ HEIGHT 6in (15cm)

☀ SPREAD 4–6in (10–15cm)

☀ SITUATION Full sun

☀ SOIL Well-drained

☀ HARDINESS Tolerates slight frost

☀ ZONES Cool-season annual in zones 2–11

**RUDBECKIA HIRTA
'MARMALADE'**
BLACK-EYED SUSAN
*Hardy annual*

This beautiful short-lived perennial is invariably grown as a hardy annual. It is distinctive and well able to create a dramatic feature, with large, brilliant golden-yellow flowers with black, conelike centers during late summer and into mid-fall.

It is ideal for filling borders with color, as well as for decorating vases indoors.

There are other varieties, in shades of yellow and mahogany.

☀ HEIGHT 2ft (60cm)

☀ SPREAD 1–1¼ ft (30–38cm)

☀ SITUATION Full sun

☀ SOIL Well-drained and light

☀ HARDINESS Tolerates slight frost

☀ ZONES 2–9 as semihardy annual

**annuals** 41

☀ ◑ ▨ ✍ ✿ ❀

**ERANTHIS HYEMALIS**
WINTER ACONITE
*Tuberous-rooted perennial*

This superb plant brings color
to gardens from midwinter to
early spring. The lemon-yellow,
buttercuplike flowers are backed by
ruffs of deeply cut green leaves.

Plant tubers 1in (2.5cm) deep and
in clusters during late summer, as
soon as they are available.

☀ HEIGHT 4in (10cm)
☀ SPREAD Space tubers 3in
(7.5cm) apart
☀ SITUATION Full sun or partial shade
☀ SOIL Well-drained but moisture-
retentive; it grows well in heavy loam
☀ HARDINESS -10° to -20°F
(-23° to -28°C)
☀ ZONES 3–7

☀ ◑ ▨ ✍ ✿ ❀

**NARCISSUS
'REMBRANDT'**
DAFFODIL
*Bulb*

A spectacular and well-known
daffodil that displays rich golden-
yellow flowers with frilled trumpets
during late winter and early spring.

It is ideal for planting in large
drifts, under deciduous trees or
in the open, to create dominant
floods of color.

Plant bulbs in late summer or
early fall, setting each bulb three
times its own depth deep.

☀ HEIGHT 1¼–1½ ft (38–45cm)
☀ SPREAD Space bulbs 3–4in
(7.5–10cm) apart
☀ SITUATION Full sun or light shade
☀ SOIL Fertile, and well-drained but
moisture-retentive
☀ HARDINESS -20° to -30°F
(-28° to -34°C)
☀ ZONES 3–9

## NARCISSUS
### 'YELLOW CHEERFULNESS'
DAFFODIL
*Bulb*

A distinctive bulbous plant, with double flowers during spring; one to three yellow flowers are produced on each stem.

Plant bulbs in late summer or early fall, setting each bulb three times its own depth deep.

* HEIGHT 1–1½ft (30–45cm)
* SPREAD Space bulbs 3–4in (7.5–10cm) apart
* SITUATION Full sun or, preferably, light shade
* SOIL Fertile, and well-drained but moisture-retentive
* HARDINESS -20° to -30°F (-28° to -34°C)
* ZONES 3–9

## TULIPA
### 'BELLONA'
SINGLE-EARLY TULIP
*Bulb*

A reliable and versatile tulip that can be planted in gardens to create a rich display in spring, or for planting in pots to flower indoors during late winter. The bright, deep yellow flowers have rounded heads.

There are many other single-early tulips, in colors including white, scarlet, red, yellow, pink, and purple.

* HEIGHT 1½ft (45cm)
* SPREAD Space bulbs 4–6in (10–15cm) apart
* SITUATION Full sun and an open position
* SOIL Fertile, and well-drained but moisture-retentive
* HARDINESS -20° to -30°F (-28° to -34°C)
* ZONES 4–7; 8–11 use as an annual

## ACHILLEA FILIPENDULINA
### 'GOLD PLATE'
**ACHILLEA EUPATORIUM**
**'GOLD PLATE'**
FERNLEAF YARROW
*Herbaceous perennial*

A distinctive border plant with
platelike heads, 4–6in (10–15cm)
wide and packed with deep yellow
flowers, from midsummer until
early fall.

Several other varieties have
golden–yellow flowers.

The flowers can be dried for
winter decoration indoors.

- ☀ **HEIGHT** 4–5ft (1.2–1.5m)
- ☀ **SPREAD** 2ft (60cm)
- ☀ **SITUATION** Full sun
- ☀ **SOIL** Well-drained but moisture-
  retentive and fertile; it dislikes
  water-logged and frozen soils
- ☀ **HARDINESS** -30° to -40°F
  (-34° to -40°C )
- ☀ **ZONES** 3–9

## ANTHEMIS TINCTORIA
GOLDEN MARGUERITE
*Herbaceous perennial*

Bushy and clump-forming, with
deeply cut green leaves and large,
daisylike, yellow to pale cream
flowers from early summer until
early fall.

There are several superb varieties,
in lemon to deep yellow, and all are
ideal in gardens. The flowers can
also be used as cut-flowers to fill
vases indoors.

- ☀ **HEIGHT** 2–2½ft (60–75cm)
- ☀ **SPREAD** 1¼–1½ft (38–45cm)
- ☀ **SITUATION** Full sun
- ☀ **SOIL** Well-drained
- ☀ **HARDINESS** 0° to -10°F (-17° to -23°C)
- ☀ **ZONES** 3–7

ACHILLEA FILIPENDULINA 'GOLD PLATE'

**AURINIA SAXATILIS**
**ALYSSUM SAXATILE**
GOLDEN TUFT
*Evergreen shrubby perennial*

With a sprawling and carpeting nature, this is ideal for clothing drystone walls, the sides of raised beds, or for bringing color to large rock gardens. Flowering extends from mid-spring to early summer.

There are several varieties, with flowers from biscuit-yellow to golden-yellow.

By cutting back shoots when flowering ceases, plants can be kept compact; it also prolongs their lives.

☀ HEIGHT 9–12in (23–30cm)
☀ SPREAD 1–1½ft (30–45cm)
☀ SITUATION Full sun
☀ SOIL Well-drained; it survives most winters, but does not tolerate a combination of low temperatures and wet soil
☀ HARDINESS -30° to -40°F (-34° to -40°C )
☀ ZONES 3–7

**COREOPSIS VERTICILLATA**
THREADLEAF COREOPSIS
*Herbaceous perennial*

A long-lived and bushy plant, with bright green, fernlike leaves and heads of star-shaped, bright yellow flowers from early summer until early fall.

Most varieties have yellow flowers, although some are deep rose-pink. For a small garden there are compact and dwarf varieties.

☀ HEIGHT 1½–1¾ft (45–50cm)
☀ SPREAD 1–1½ft (30–45cm)
☀ SITUATION Full sun or light, partial shade
☀ SOIL Light, but moisture-retentive; it dislikes frozen and wet soils
☀ HARDINESS 0° to -10°F (-17° to -23°C)
☀ ZONES 3–9

**EUPHORBIA POLYCHROMA**
**EUPHORBIA EPITHYMOIDES**
*Hardy, subshrubby evergreen*

This evergreen is bushy and clump-forming, with rich green leaves and clustered heads of bright yellow bracts during mid- and late spring.

Although it has a subshrubby nature, cut all stems to ground level in fall or spring in order to keep plants bushy.

☀ HEIGHT 1½ft (45cm)

☀ SPREAD 1–2ft (30–60cm)

☀ SITUATION Full sun

☀ SOIL Well-drained and relatively light; it dislikes heavy, wet, and cold soils

☀ HARDINESS 0° to -10°F
   (-17° to -23°C)

☀ ZONES 4–8

**HELIANTHUS**
**'LODDON GOLD'**
**HELIANTHUS DECAPETALUS**
**'LODDON GOLD'**
THIN-LEAF SUNFLOWER
*Herbaceous perennial*

Bushy and clump-forming, with upright stems bearing mid-green, rough-surfaced, and sharply toothed-edged leaves. From midsummer to early fall these hardy plants create dominant displays of golden-yellow, daisylike flowers, each being 2–3in (5–7.5cm) wide.

Insert twiggy pea-sticks around plants when still small to support tall growth later in the summer.

☀ HEIGHT 4–5ft (1.2–1.5m)

☀ SPREAD 1½–2ft (45–60cm)

☀ SITUATION Bright and sunny

☀ SOIL Well-drained

☀ HARDINESS -10° to -20°F
   (-23° to -28°C)

☀ ZONES 6–9

**HEMEROCALLIS
'STELLA DE ORO'**
DAYLILY
*Herbaceous perennial*

This forms a stocky clump of grass-green leaves and a continuous display of bell-shaped, canary yellow flowers with orange throats, from early to late summer.

The range of species and hybrids is wide and includes colors such as pink, red, and purple.

The plants do not need to be supported. Cut the stems almost to soil level after their flowers fade.

✳ **HEIGHT** 22in (55cm)

✳ **SPREAD** 1½ft (45cm)

✳ **SITUATION** Full sun or light shade

✳ **SOIL** Fertile and well-drained

✳ **HARDINESS** -20° to -30°F (-28° to -34°C)

✳ **ZONES** 3–10

**LIGULARIA
'THE ROCKET'**
SENECIO PRZEWALSKII
'THE ROCKET'
*Hardy herbaceous perennial*

A spectacular plant, with an upright stance and large, deeply incised basal leaves. During mid- and late summer tall, black stems produce long spires, which are up to 2ft (60cm) long and are packed with dark yellow flowers.

✳ **HEIGHT** 5–6ft (1.5–1.8m)

✳ **SPREAD** 2–2½ft (60–75cm)

✳ **SITUATION** Partial shade; it will grow in full sun, but the roots must be kept cool and moist

✳ **SOIL** Fertile and moisture-retentive; water the soil thoroughly in summer, and mulch the surface in late spring

✳ **HARDINESS** -20° to -30°F- (28° to -34°C)

✳ **ZONES** 5–8

HEMEROCALLIS 'STELLA DE ORO'

47

POTENTILLA
'YELLOW QUEEN'
CINQUEFOIL
*Herbaceous perennial*

With a sprawling, irregular shape and strawberrylike leaves, this attractive plant bears semidouble, saucer-shaped, bright yellow flowers in loose sprays from early summer to fall.

Other varieties extend the color range to bright red, scarlet, crimson-maroon, and orange.

These are ideal border plants and seldom fail to create a distinctive display there.

* HEIGHT 1¼ft (38cm)
* SPREAD 1¼ft (38cm)
* SITUATION Full sun
* SOIL Well-drained but moisture-retentive
* HARDINESS -10° to -20°F (-23° to -28°C)
* ZONES 5–8

RUDBECKIA FULGIDA
'GOLDSTURM'
RUDBECKIA SPECIOSA
'GOLDSTURM'
SHOWY CONEFLOWER
*Herbaceous perennial*

A bushy and clump-forming plant, with oblong to lance-shaped green leaves and large yellow flowers, up to 5in (13cm) wide and with dark brown, conelike centers, from mid-summer to early fall.

Lift and divide congested plants every three or four years; replant young pieces from around the outside of the clump.

* HEIGHT 2–3ft (60–90cm)
* SPREAD 1½–2ft (45–60cm)
* SITUATION Sunny and open
* SOIL Well-drained but moisture-retentive
* HARDINESS -20° to -30°F (-28° to -34°C)
* ZONES 3–9

### SOLIDAGO
### 'CROWN OF RAYS'
GOLDENROD
*Herbaceous perennial*

A bushy border plant with upright stems bearing clusters of fluffy, plumelike heads packed with rich yellow flowers from midsummer to mid-fall. It seldom fails to create a spectacular display.

There are many other garden hybrids, in several heights, but all in shades of yellow.

- ☀ HEIGHT 1½–2ft (45–60cm)
- ☀ SPREAD 1–1¼ft (30–38cm)
- ☀ SITUATION Full sun or light shade
- ☀ SOIL Ordinary, and well-drained but moisture-retentive
- ☀ HARDINESS -20° to -30°F (-28° to -34°C)
- ☀ ZONES 3–9

### TROLLIUS EUROPAEUS
COMMON GLOBEFLOWER
*Herbaceous perennial*

A distinctive plant, with deeply cleft and lobed, deep green leaves and upright stems. They bear large, globular, buttercuplike, rich golden-yellow flowers up to 2in (5cm) wide during late spring and early summer.

There are several varieties, in colors ranging from yellow and cream to orange.

- ☀ HEIGHT 1½–2ft (45–60cm)
- ☀ SPREAD 1½ft (45cm)
- ☀ SITUATION Full sun or partial shade
- ☀ SOIL Fertile and moisture-retentive; moisture is essential, so mix peat or well-decayed garden compost into the soil; water the soil and apply a mulch in spring
- ☀ HARDINESS -10° to -20°F (-23° to -28°C )
- ☀ ZONES 4–7

## BUDDLEJA × WEYERIANA 'SUNGOLD'
### BUDDLEIA × WEYERIANA 'SUNGOLD'
*Deciduous shrub*

A distinctive and vigorous hybrid, bearing ball-shaped heads of orange-yellow flowers, often tinged with mauve and borne in long, slender clusters, from early summer to fall.

It is a hybrid between *Buddleja alternifolia* and *B. globosa*, the well-known orange-ball tree.

No regular pruning is needed, other than occasionally cutting out misplaced and dead shoots during the spring.

☀ HEIGHT 6–10ft (1.8–3m)

☀ SPREAD 6–8ft (1.8–2.4m)

☀ SITUATION Full sun and shelter from cold wind

☀ SOIL Light, and well-drained but moisture-retentive

☀ HARDINESS 0° to -10°F (-17° to -23°C)

☀ ZONES 7–9

## CYTISUS × KEWENSIS
### BROOM
*Deciduous shrub*

A low, spreading, and arching shrub with small, mid-green leaves and stems festooned with pale yellow, ½in (12mm) long flowers during late spring.

It is ideal for planting in a large rock garden, or near the edge of a raised bed.

After the flowers fade, cut off two-thirds of all shoots. This encourages the growth of shoots that will bear flowers during the following spring.

☀ HEIGHT 1–2ft (30–60cm)

☀ SPREAD 3¼–4ft (1–1.2m)

☀ SITUATION Full sun

☀ SOIL Well-drained

☀ HARDINESS 0° to -10°F (-17° to -23°C)

☀ ZONES 5–8

## FORSYTHIA 'BEATRIX FARRAND'

FORSYTHIA × 'BEATRIX FARRAND'
*Deciduous shrub*

A spectacular shrub with rich yellow flowers, about 1½in (36mm) across, packed on leafless stems during early and mid-spring. The mid-green, prominently toothed leaves appear in late spring.

Regular pruning is essential; use sharp pruners to cut out old and damaged shoots as soon as the flowers fade. Also shorten any vigorous shoots.

☀ HEIGHT 6–8ft (1.8–2.4m)

☀ SPREAD 5–7ft (1.5–2.1m)

☀ SITUATION Full sun or partial shade

☀ SOIL Ordinary, and well-drained but moisture-retentive

☀ HARDINESS -10° to -20°F (-23° to -28°C)

☀ ZONES 5–8

## FREMONTODENDRON CALIFORNICUM

FREMONTIA CALIFORNICA
*Deciduous or semievergreen shrub*

A slightly tender shrub usually grown against a sunny, wind-sheltered wall, where from late spring to fall it reveals golden-yellow, cup-shaped flowers, each up to 2in (5cm) wide. The dull green, somewhat ivylike leaves have three to seven lobes.

No regular pruning is needed, other than cutting out damaged shoots in spring.

☀ HEIGHT 8–10ft (2.4–3m)

☀ SPREAD 6–8ft (1.8–2.4m)

☀ SITUATION Full sun and shelter from cold wind

☀ SOIL Well-drained and light

☀ HARDINESS 0° to -10°F (-17° to -23°C)

☀ ZONES 7–10

### GENISTA AETNENSIS
MT ETNA BROOM
*Deciduous shrub*

An erect and tall shrub, often
having the nature of a small tree,
with a sparse habit and slender,
rushlike, bright green branches that
bear golden-yellow, pea-shaped
flowers in 3–4in (7.5–10cm) long
terminal clusters during mid- and
late summer.

No regular pruning is needed.

❄ HEIGHT 15–20ft (4.5–6m)

❄ SPREAD 15–18ft (4.5–5.4m)

❄ SITUATION Full sun

❄ SOIL Light and well-drained

❄ HARDINESS 20° to 10°F
(-6° to -12°C)

❄ ZONES 6–9

### HYPERICUM 'HIDCOTE'
HYPERICUM PATULUM 'HIDCOTE'
*Evergreen or semievergreen shrub*

A spectacular shrub, mostly
evergreen except in very cold areas,
with dark green leaves and masses
of shallowly saucer-shaped, golden-
yellow flowers up to 3in (7.5cm)
across, from midsummer until
the fall.

No regular pruning is needed,
other than shortening some of the
previous year's shoots in spring. In
cold areas, young shoots become
damaged by severe frost.

❄ HEIGHT 4–5ft (1.2–1.5m)

❄ SPREAD 5–8ft (1.5–2.4m)

❄ SITUATION Full sun

❄ SOIL Fertile and well-drained

❄ HARDINESS 10° to 0°F
(-12° to -17°C)

❄ ZONES 6–9

## KERRIA JAPONICA
### 'PLENIFLORA'
KERRIA
*Deciduous shrub*

This shrub is bushy, with slender, glossy green, erect stems that bear bright green, tooth-edged leaves. During mid- and late spring, these stems become peppered with double, bright orange–yellow flowers, each of which is 1½–2in (36–50mm) wide.

Regular pruning encourages the yearly development of flowers: after the flowers fade, thin out shoots to encourage the development of fresh shoots from ground level.

❊ HEIGHT 8–12ft (2.4–3.6m)
❊ SPREAD 4–5ft (1.2–1.5m)
❊ SITUATION Full sun or partial shade
❊ SOIL Well-drained
❊ HARDINESS -20° to -30°F (-28° to -34°C)
❊ ZONES 4–9

## MAHONIA JAPONICA
### 'BEALEI'
MAHONIA BEALEI
*Evergreen shrub*

An upright shrub with leathery, gray-green, stiff leaves with attractive yellow-green undersides. During mid- and late winter it bears lemon-yellow flowers in stiff, upright clusters, about 4–6in (10–15cm) long, at the tips of its stems.

No regular pruning is needed.

❊ HEIGHT 6–7ft (1.8–2.1m)
❊ SPREAD 6–7ft (1.8–2.1m)
❊ SITUATION Light, dappled shade
❊ SOIL Moisture-retentive, leafy, and light, and neutral to slightly acid
❊ HARDINESS 0° to -10°F (-17° to -23°C)
❊ ZONES 7–9

JERUSALEM SAGE
*Evergreen shrub*

A shrubby plant, with an untidy, sprawling nature and gray–green, woolly, wedge-shaped leaves. Whorls of hooded, tubular, stalkless, bright yellow flowers appear during early and midsummer. It is ideal for growing in a mixed border.

No regular pruning is needed, other than cutting out frosted and misplaced stems after the flowers have faded.

❋ HEIGHT 3–4ft (90cm–1.2m)

❋ SPREAD 2–3ft (60–90cm)

❋ SITUATION Full sun, and shelter from cold wind

❋ SOIL Light and well-drained

❋ HARDINESS 10° to 0°F (-12° to -17°C)

❋ ZONES 5–8

AZALEA PONTICA/
RHODODENDRON FLAVUM
*Deciduous shrub*

A rather stiff-stemmed, vigorous shrub with funnel-shaped, fragrant, rich yellow flowers borne in rounded trusses on naked branches during mid- and late spring. The winter buds and young shoots are sticky, while the 2½–4in (6–10cm) long, matt green leaves assume rich shades of purple, crimson, and yellow in fall.

No regular pruning is needed.

❋ HEIGHT 6–8ft (1.8–2.4m)

❋ SPREAD 5–7ft (1.5–2.1m)

❋ SITUATION Lightly shaded and sheltered from cold wind

❋ SOIL Neutral or slightly acid; mix peat or leafmold into the soil

❋ HARDINESS -10° to -20°F (-23° to -28°C)

❋ ZONES 5–8

**ROSA XANTHINA**
**'CANARY BIRD'**
MANCHU ROSE
*Deciduous shrub*

A distinctive rose with brown, arching stems bearing triangular prickles and dainty, fernlike yellow leaves formed of seven to thirteen leaflets. During late spring and early summer it bears bright golden-yellow, semidouble flowers about 2in (5cm) wide. Sometimes flowers also appear in fall.

Occasionally, cut out old and dead wood in fall, to allow light and air to enter the shrub.

❋ HEIGHT 6–7ft (1.8–2.1m)
❋ SPREAD 7–8ft (2.1–2.4m)
❋ SITUATION Full sun, away from overhanging trees
❋ SOIL Well-drained but moisture-retentive; mix in well-decomposed compost
❋ HARDINESS -10° to -20°F (-23° to -28°C)
❋ ZONES 5–8

**STACHYURUS PRAECOX**
*Deciduous shrub*

An attractive shrub, with arching branches bearing pale yellow flowers in catkinlike clusters, up to 4in (10cm) long, from late winter to mid-spring. These appear before the slender-pointed, mid-green leaves. The catkins are especially attractive when highlighted against a blue sky.

No special pruning is needed, other than occasionally cutting out damaged or misplaced branches.

❋ HEIGHT 8–10ft (2.4–3m)
❋ SPREAD 8–10ft (2.4–3m)
❋ SITUATION Full sun or partial shade, and shelter from cold wind
❋ SOIL Well-drained but moisture-retentive; mix in well-decomposed compost
❋ HARDINESS 10° to 0°F (-12° to -17°C)
❋ ZONES 6–8

**CLEMATIS ORIENTALIS**
ORANGE-PEEL CLEMATIS
*Deciduous climber*

A vigorous climber, forming a
tangled mass of slender shoots
clothed in light green, fernlike
leaves. Nodding, starlike, and yellow
flowers, each about 1½in (36mm)
wide, appear from late summer to
mid-fall. These are then followed
by silvery gray, silky seedheads.

Regular pruning is not necessary.
However, where plants become too
large, cut out excessive growth in
the spring.

* HEIGHT 10–20ft (3–6m)
* SPREAD 10–20ft (3–6m)
* SITUATION Open and sunny, but
  the base of the climber should be
  shaded from strong, direct sunlight
* SOIL Fertile, slightly alkaline, and
  well-drained
* HARDINESS 0° to -10°F
  (-17° to -23°C)
* ZONES 6–9

**ROSA BANKSIAE**
**'LUTEA'**
YELLOW BANKS ROSE
*Semievergreen climbing shrub*

A climbing species rose, with
slender, almost thornless, strong,
and arching stems that bear clusters
of small, double, slightly fragrant
yellow flowers during late spring
and early summer.

Prune the shoots only lightly,
because severe pruning encourages
vigorous growth.

* HEIGHT 20ft (6m)
* SPREAD 8–10ft (2.4–3m)
* SITUATION Warm and sheltered
* SOIL Well-drained but
  moisture-retentive
* HARDINESS 10° to 0°F
  (-12° to -17°C)
* ZONES 7–8

**PYRACANTHA
'SOLEIL D'OR'**
FIRETHORN
*Evergreen shrub*

A spectacular hardy shrub with a spreading habit and thorny branches packed with dark green leaves. White flowers appear in early summer and are later followed by masses of deep golden-yellow, berrylike fruits.

Other pyracanthas have attractive berries, which range in color from bright red to orange, as well as yellow.

No regular pruning is needed.

☀ **HEIGHT** 8ft (2.4m)
☀ **SPREAD** 10ft (3m)
☀ **SITUATION** Full sun or partial shade
☀ **SOIL** Fertile and well-drained
☀ **HARDINESS** 20° to 10°F
    (-6° to -12°C)
☀ **ZONES** 6–9

**VIBURNUM OPULUS
'XANTHOCARPUM'**
EUROPEAN CRANBERRY-BUSH
*Deciduous shrub*

A large, bushy, and upright shrub with gray stems bearing dark green, maplelike leaves and white, heavily scented flowers in 2–3in (5–7.5cm) wide, flat heads during early summer; sometimes they appear in midsummer. These are followed in fall by golden-yellow, berrylike fruits, which become translucent as they ripen.

Other forms of this shrub have red berries.

No regular pruning is needed, but thin out congested shrubs as soon as the flowers fade.

☀ **HEIGHT** 10–15ft (3–4.5m)
☀ **SPREAD** 12–15ft (3.6–4.5m)
☀ **SITUATION** Full sun and shelter
    from strong, cold wind
☀ **SOIL** Fertile, and moisture-retentive
    but well-drained
☀ **HARDINESS** -30° to -40°F
    (-34° to -40°C)
☀ **ZONES** 3–8

## HOSTA
### 'SUN POWER'
PLANTAIN-LILY
*Herbaceous perennial*

This quick-growing border plant forms a graceful clump with golden, slightly twisted leaves that keep their color right through to the frosts of fall.

Pale lavender flowers appear in late summer.

- ☀ HEIGHT 2–2½ft (60–75cm)
- ☀ SPREAD 2½–3ft (75–90cm)
- ☀ SITUATION Full shade to about three-quarters sun
- ☀ SOIL Fertile, and moisture-retentive but well-drained
- ☀ HARDINESS 0° to -10°F (-17° to -23°C)
- ☀ ZONES 3–9

## LYSIMACHIA NUMMULARIA
### 'AUREA'
YELLOW MONEYWORT
*Evergreen perennial*

A creeping, ground-hugging plant with trailing stems bearing bright yellow leaves and golden, cup-shaped flowers about ½in (12mm) across during early and midsummer.

It is an ideal perennial for planting at the edge of an informal garden pond. However, it is an adaptable plant and will also grow in dry soil in a border.

- ☀ HEIGHT 2–3in (5–7.5cm)
- ☀ SPREAD 9–18in (23–45cm)
- ☀ SITUATION Full sun or partial shade
- ☀ SOIL Preferably moist, but also grows in drier conditions
- ☀ HARDINESS -20° to -30°F (-28° to -34°C)
- ☀ ZONES 3–8

**'AUREUM'**
GOLDEN MILLET
*Perennial grass*

A perennial that forms loose tufts of evergreen, pale golden–yellow to lime–green leaves about 1ft (30cm) high. It also develops delicate clusters of flowers on stems about 2ft (60cm) high.

Increase this attractive grass by lifting and dividing congested clumps in spring. It can also be raised from seed.

☀ HEIGHT 1–2ft (30–60cm)

☀ SPREAD 10–12in (25–30cm)

☀ SITUATION Full sun or light, dappled shade

☀ SOIL Fertile, and moisture-retentive but well-drained

☀ HARDINESS 0° to -10°F (-17° to -23°C)

☀ ZONES 6–8

ORIGANUM VULGARE
**'AUREUM'**
YELLOW-LEAVED MARJORAM
*Perennial*

This colorful form of the common marjoram creates a mass of golden–yellow leaves; these are especially attractive when young and during the early part of the year. As the season progresses, they become greenish-yellow.

Trim back plants in late summer or early fall.

☀ HEIGHT 6–8in (15–20cm)

☀ SPREAD 10–12in (25–30cm)

☀ SITUATION Full sun

☀ SOIL Well-drained but moisture-retentive

☀ HARDINESS -10° to -20°F- (23° to -28°C)

☀ ZONES 5–9

ORIGANUM VULGARE 'AUREUM'

CALLUNA VULGARIS
**'GOLD HAZE'**
HEATHER
*Evergreen shrub*

A low-growing and ground-hugging shrub with bright golden-yellow foliage throughout the year and masses of white flowers during late summer and early fall.

This makes an ideal shrub for blanketing the ground, as well as for creating color contrasts with blue- and green-leaved dwarf and slow-growing conifers.

☀ HEIGHT 1½–2ft (45–60cm)

☀ SPREAD 2–2½ft (60–75cm)

☀ SITUATION Open and sunny position, away from deciduous trees that may shed leaves over them in fall

☀ SOIL Well-drained but moisture-retentive, and neutral or slightly acid; it will not grow in limy soil

☀ HARDINESS -20° to -30°F (-28° to -34°C)

☀ ZONES 4–6

LONICERA NITIDA
**'BAGGESEN'S GOLD'**
GOLDEN-LEAVED BOX HONEYSUCKLE
*Evergreen shrub*

An attractive, dense, and bushy shrub packed with small, golden leaves throughout the year. Although sometimes grown as a formal hedge and regularly clipped, it is superb when grown to create a freestanding, irregularly shaped bush. Alternatively, plant it to screen a wall or fence.

☀ HEIGHT 5–6ft (1.5–1.8m)

☀ SPREAD 5–6ft (1.5–1.8m)

☀ SITUATION Full sun or partial shade

☀ SOIL Light, and well-drained but moisture-retentive

☀ HARDINESS 10° to 0°F (-12° to -17°C)

☀ ZONES 7–9

**PHILADELPHUS CORONARIUS**
**'AUREUS'**
**PHILADELPHUS CORONARIUS**
**'FOLIIS AUREIS'**
YELLOW-LEAVED SWEET MOCK-ORANGE
*Deciduous shrub*

An exceptionally attractive, upright shrub with bright golden-yellow leaves in spring. By midsummer they start to lose their brightness and become greenish-yellow.

No regular pruning is needed, other than occasionally thinning out old shoots to encourage the development of young ones.

❊ HEIGHT 6–7ft (1.8–2.1m)
❊ SPREAD 5–7ft (1.5–2.1m)
❊ SITUATION Shade or light shade helps the leaves to retain their color
❊ SOIL Well-drained
❊ HARDINESS -10° to -20°F (-23° to -28°C)
❊ ZONES 4–8

**PHYSOCARPUS OPULIFOLIUS**
**'LUTEUS'**
SPIRAEA OPULIFOLIA 'AUREUS'
YELLOW-LEAVED EASTERN NINEBARK
*Deciduous shrub*

A spectacular shrub, often large and dominant, with three-lobed, golden-yellow leaves. These are especially attractive when young; gradually they become greener.

During early summer it bears 2in (5cm) wide clusters of white flowers tinged with rose. Additionally, the bark peels and is attractive in winter.

❊ HEIGHT 6–8ft (1.8–2.4m)
❊ SPREAD 5–7ft (1.5–2.1m)
❊ SITUATION Full sun
❊ SOIL Moisture-retentive but well-drained
❊ HARDINESS -40° to -50°F (-40° to -45°C)
❊ ZONES 2–7

SAMBUCUS RACEMOSA
**'PLUMOSA AUREA'**
SAMBUCUS RACEMOSA
**'SERRATIFOLIA AUREA'**
EUROPEAN RED ELDER
*Deciduous shrub*

An exceptionally attractive, slow-growing shrub, which becomes a bright beacon throughout summer; it reveals deeply divided, finely cut golden leaves. During spring it develops fluffy, pyramidal heads of yellowish-white flowers.

To create a smaller shrub with more brilliant foliage, cut back the stems to near soil level in spring.

☀ HEIGHT 7–10ft (2.1–3m)
☀ SPREAD 7–10ft (2.1–3m)
☀ SITUATION In a bright, sunny position the leaves are attractive earlier than when planted in shade; however, a cool, moist situation ensures the color remains brighter for longer
☀ SOIL Fertile, and moisture-retentive but well-drained
☀ HARDINESS -20° to -30°F (-28° to -34°C)
☀ ZONES 3–7

SPIRAEA JAPONICA
**'GOLDFLAME'**
SPIRAEA × BUMALDA 'GOLDFLAME'
*Deciduous shrub*

A bushy, clump-forming shrub that is outstandingly attractive in spring, when the young leaves are gold and flame-colored. Later they become light green.

Deep rosy red flowers appear in flat heads, up to 5in (13cm) across, during mid- and late summer.

To encourage the development of fresh shoots, cut back all stems to 3–4in (7.5–10cm) above the ground during late winter or early spring.

☀ HEIGHT 2½ft (75cm)
☀ SPREAD 2½–3ft (75–90cm)
☀ SITUATION Full sun
☀ SOIL Light, fertile, and moisture-retentive
☀ HARDINESS -10° to -20°F (-23° to -28°C)
☀ ZONES 3–8

CAREX ELATA
'AUREA'
CAREX ACUTA 'AUREOVARIEGATA'
VARIEGATED TUFTED SEDGE
*Hardy sedge*

A beautiful tufted sedge, forming a dense tussock of narrow green leaves with golden-yellow edges.

There are several other sedges with colored or variegated leaves, including *C. elata* 'Bowles' Golden', which reveals golden-yellow leaves with green edges, and *C. elata* 'Knightshayes' with yellow leaves.

☀ HEIGHT 1–3ft (30–90cm)

☀ SPREAD 1–2ft (30–60cm)

☀ SITUATION Light shade

☀ SOIL Preferably moisture-retentive, although plants will grow in moderately dry soil in borders; generally, it grows larger in moist soil

☀ HARDINESS 10° to 0°F (-12° to -17°C)

☀ ZONES 5–9

IRIS PSEUDACORUS
'VARIEGATA'
VARIEGATED YELLOW FLAG IRIS
*Water-loving herbaceous iris*

A distinctive and hardy water plant, which is ideal for planting at a pond's edge. It develops erect, swordlike, bluish-green leaves with yellow stripes. During early summer it bears 3in (7.5cm) wide yellow flowers, followed by brown seed capsules.

In fall, cut down the leaves and stems and remove them from the pond; if left in the water they decompose and cause toxic gases.

☀ HEIGHT 2½–3ft (75–90cm)

☀ SPREAD 1¼–1½ft (38–45cm)

☀ SITUATION Full sun or light shade

☀ SOIL Fertile, and in water 6in (15cm) deep

☀ HARDINESS 30° to 20°F (-1° to -6°C)

☀ ZONES 3–9

An attractive form of the
well-known balm, but with fragrant
gold-and-green leaves borne
on upright stems.

To encourage the development
of attractively variegated leaves, cut
back all stems to 6in (15cm) above
the ground during early summer;
additionally, cut plants to ground
level in fall.

❋ HEIGHT 2–3ft (60–90cm)

❋ SPREAD 1–1½ft (30–45cm)

❋ SITUATION Full sun

❋ SOIL Light, and moisture-retentive but
well-drained

❋ HARDINESS -20° to -30°F
(-28° to -34°C)

❋ ZONES 4–9

MENTHA × GRACILIS
**'VARIEGATA'**
MENTHA × GRACILIS 'AUREA'
MENTHA × GENTILIS 'VARIEGATA'
VARIEGATED MINT
*Herbaceous perennial*

A quick-growing, invasive, and
spreading mint with red-purple
stems and oval to lance-shaped
mid-green, fragrant leaves that are
boldly splashed with yellow. From
midsummer to early fall it produces
pale purple, tubular flowers; these
are best pinched off.

❋ HEIGHT 1–1½ft (30–45cm)

❋ SPREAD 1–1½ft (30–45cm)

❋ SITUATION Partially shaded

❋ SOIL Well-drained but moisture-
retentive

❋ HARDINESS 0° to -10°F
(-17° to -23°C)

❋ ZONES 5–8

**AUCUBA JAPONICA
'VARIEGATA'**
**AUCUBA JAPONICA 'MACULATA'**
JAPANESE AUCUBA
*Evergreen shrub*

A rounded and dense shrub with shiny, leathery, dark green leaves irregularly spotted with yellow. It is attractive throughout the year, but especially in winter when the leaves are highlighted by low rays from the sun. Plant daffodils around it for extra color in spring.

☀ HEIGHT 5–8ft (1.5–2.4m)

☀ SPREAD 5–8ft (1.5–2.4m)

☀ SITUATION Full sun or light shade

☀ SOIL Well-drained but moisture-retentive

☀ HARDINESS 10° to 0°F
    (-12° to -17°C)

☀ ZONES 7–10

**CORNUS ALBA
'SPAETHII'**
DOGWOOD
*Deciduous shrub*

A slightly sprawling and suckering shrub with red bark in winter and glorious golden-edged, variegated leaves throughout summer. It has the virtue of its golden coloring not being scorched or faded by hot sun.

Additionally, the colorful stems look attractive in winter when caught by the sun's low rays.

Where this shrub is mainly grown for its colorful stems, cut the entire plant to near soil level in mid-spring.

☀ HEIGHT 6–9ft (1.8–2.7m)

☀ SPREAD 6–9ft (1.8–2.7m)

☀ SITUATION Full sun or light shade

☀ SOIL Well-drained but moisture-retentive

☀ HARDINESS -30° to -40°F
    (-34° to -40°C)

☀ ZONES 2–7

### ELAEAGNUS PUNGENS 'MACULATA'
THORNY ELAEAGNUS
*Evergreen shrub*

A spreading shrub, with a rounded
outline and thorny stems bearing
oval, leathery, glossy–green leaves
splashed with gold. It creates a
beacon of color throughout the
year. Silvery white, fragrant flowers
appear in fall.

Occasionally, all–green shoots
appear; if this happens, cut them
completely out.

- ☼ HEIGHT 6–10ft (1.8–3m)
- ☼ SPREAD 6–10ft (1.8–3m)
- ☼ SITUATION Full sun or partial shade
- ☼ SOIL Well-drained but moisture-
  retentive
- ☼ HARDINESS 10° to 0°F
  (-12° to -17°C)
- ☼ ZONES 6–9

### ILEX AQUIFOLIUM 'AUREO-MARGINATA'
VARIEGATED ENGLISH HOLLY
*Evergreen shrub*

This holly has stiff, thick, and
leathery green leaves with gold
edges. The female form bears
clusters of red berries, which persist
throughout much of the winter.

There are many other hollies with
yellow variegated leaves; some are
almost spineless, whereas others are
sharp in their prickliness.

No regular pruning is needed,
other than occasionally cutting out
a misplaced branch in spring.

- ☼ HEIGHT 10–12ft (3–3.6m)
- ☼ SPREAD 8–10ft (2.4–3m)
- ☼ SITUATION Full sun or light shade
- ☼ SOIL Well-drained but moisture-
  retentive
- ☼ HARDINESS 0° to -10°F
  (-17° to -23°C)
- ☼ ZONES 6–9

**ARUNDINARIA AURICOMA**
GOLDEN-HAIRED BAMBOO
*Bamboo*

A colorful dwarf bamboo forming a thicket of erect, slender, purplish–green canes and pea-green leaves almost entirely striped in yellow.

This bamboo is still listed in some catalogues as *Arundinaria viridistriata* or *Pleioblastus viridistriatus*.

✴ HEIGHT 3–4ft (90cm–1.2m)

✴ SPREAD 3–4ft (90cm–1.2m)

✴ SITUATION Full sun or partial shade; shelter from cold wind is beneficial

✴ SOIL Moisture-retentive but well-drained

✴ HARDINESS 10° to 0°F (-12° to -17°C)

✴ ZONES 7–10

**SALVIA OFFICINALIS**
**'ICTERINA'**
VARIEGATED SAGE
*Evergreen shrub*

A richly colored and relatively short-lived, slightly tender shrub, which in cold regions may become semievergreen. Nevertheless, its green–and–gold variegated leaves make it a superb garden plant.

Other ornamental sages include 'Purpurescens' (young leaves suffused with purple) and 'Tricolor' (gray-green leaves that are splashed creamy-white and suffused with pink and purple).

✴ HEIGHT 1½–2ft (45–60cm)

✴ SPREAD 1½–2ft (45–60cm)

✴ SITUATION Full sun or light shade; shelter from cold wind is beneficial

✴ SOIL Well-drained but moisture-retentive

✴ HARDINESS -10° to -20°F (-23° to -28°C)

✴ ZONES 4–9

*PLEIOBLASTUS AURICOMUS*

**shrubs with variegated foliage** 67

*A yellow border brings life to any garden.*

# index for yellow

*See the following pages for other plants with several varieties, including yellow:*

HELIANTHUS ANNUUS

# ORANGE

*The bright glow of orange is a positive tonic for a quiet spring day, although it is found in relatively few plants.*

# the color orange
# orange plants

There are relatively few orange flowers for temperate gardens—perhaps because it does not always appear an attractive color under dull northern skies. In the brighter skies of Australia and South Africa there is a much wider range of orange plants, most of which come alive in bright sunlight. Despite this limitation there are still some exciting orange flowers from which to choose, including a range of colors, from the scarlet-orange of most of the crocosmias to the true orange of *Geum* 'Borisii' and *Calendula officinalis* and the yellow-orange of many *Tagetes*. Tints of orange are seen in *Chrysanthemum* 'Apricot' and, even paler tints, in *Hyacinthus orientalis* 'Gipsy Queen'; there are also several striking terra cotta-colored flowers, including *Helenium* 'Moerheim Beauty' and *Euphorbia griffithii* 'Fireglow'.

The orange flowers of Helianthemum nummularium 'Fire Dragon' are seen at their best in bright sunlight.

## COLOR HARMONIES

Orange does not harmonize naturally with the bright green of many leaves and, to be used successfully, much of the green foliage needs to be replaced with either dark green or plum foliage. The adjacent colors to orange are red and yellow—all three colors can be used together, but it may be more satisfactory using just two of them: try a mixture of orange and yellow marigolds for an orange-yellow harmony. Fall is a good time of year to try orange and red as adjacent colors,

either in a planting of shrubs for fall color or in a border of orange and red flowers together (in the section on color schemes we have included a "hot" color scheme for the fall [*see p.24*]; try adding a few red flowers to the list). The opposite and complementary color to orange is

*The orange foliage of Japanese maples strikingly offsets other garden features.*

blue—imagine bright orange fall leaves against a bright blue sky or, more immediately, imagine a blue glass bowl heaped full of tangerines! This is quite a difficult harmony to use in the garden, due to the abundance of green as an unwanted third color, but try adding blue flowers and berries to your fall-colored border for maximum impact.

## USING ORANGE IN YOUR GARDEN

Orange is possibly at its best when isolated from other colors. If you plant a container with a mass of *Tulipa* 'Oranje Nassau' so that the flowers are almost touching you can see what we mean: it really glows. Paint the container blue and you have the outdoor equivalent of the blue bowl of tangerines! Another great combination is to plant orange crocosmias and phygelius in front of the plum-colored leaves of *Cotinus coggygria* 'Royal Purple', with perhaps an edging of the similarly colored leaves of *Heuchera micrantha* 'Palace Purple' in front. This is a form of red-orange harmony, but using shades of red rather than the full hue or tints.

ALSTROEMERIA AUREA 'DOVER ORANGE'

71

## CALENDULA OFFICINALIS
POT-MARIGOLD
*Hardy annual*

A popular hardy annual, previously used medicinally, with a bushy and upright stance. It has light green, long and narrow, fragrant leaves and large, petal-packed, daisylike, bright yellow or orange flowers.

There are double-flowered and dwarf varieties, in colors including yellow, orange, and reddish-orange.

❋ HEIGHT 1½–2ft (45–60cm)

❋ SPREAD 1–1¼ft (30–38cm)

❋ SITUATION Full sun

❋ SOIL Grows well in poor soil, although well-drained but moisture-retentive conditions are best

❋ HARDINESS Tolerates slight frost

❋ ZONES Cool-season annual in zones 2–11

## ERYSIMUM CHEIRI 'ORANGE BEDDER'
CHEIRANTHUS CHEIRI
'ORANGE BEDDER'
COMMON WALLFLOWER
*Biennial*

This well-known hardy perennial is invariably grown as a hardy biennial for flowering during late spring and early summer. 'Orange Bedder', with its dense spikes of richly scented orange flowers, is a dwarf variety.

❋ HEIGHT 9–12in (23–30cm)

❋ SPREAD 8–10in (20–25cm)

❋ SITUATION Full sun

❋ SOIL Fertile, well-drained, and slightly alkaline

❋ HARDINESS Tolerates temperatures down to about 20°F (-6°C)

❋ ZONES Biennial, grown as an annual in cold winter zones

CALENDULA OFFICINALIS

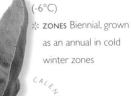

## ESCHSCHOLZIA CALIFORNICA
CALIFORNIA-POPPY
*Hardy annual*

This brightly colored hardy annual creates a wealth of delicate, finely cut, blue-green leaves and masses of saucer-shaped, bright orange-yellow flowers, each up to 3in (7.5cm) wide, from early to late summer.

The flowers are followed by beautiful 3–4in (7.5–10cm) long blue-green seedpods.

A range of varieties extends the color range to scarlet, crimson, rose, orange, yellow, white, and red.

☀ HEIGHT 1–1¼ft (30–38cm)

☀ SPREAD 6–9in (15–23cm)

☀ SITUATION Full sun

☀ SOIL Light, poor, and well-drained; when grown in fertile and heavy soil the quality of color diminishes

☀ HARDINESS Tolerates slight frost

☀ ZONES Cool-season annual in zones 2–11

## GAZANIA 'DAYBREAK BRIGHT ORANGE'
TREASURE FLOWER
*Semihardy annual*

A tender perennial, usually grown as a half-hardy annual. It develops dark green, lance-shaped leaves with gray undersides, and from midsummer to the frosts of fall creates a wealth of 3in (7.5cm) wide, daisylike, bright orange flowers. Incidentally, the flowers close in the evening.

There are several superb varieties, and colors include yellow, orange, red, pink, brown, and ruby.

☀ HEIGHT 9in (23cm)

☀ SPREAD 9–12in (23–30cm)

☀ SITUATION Full sun

☀ SOIL Well-drained and light

☀ HARDINESS Will not tolerate temperatures below 32°F (0°C)

☀ ZONES Tender annual in zones 2–8; perennial in zones 9–11

**MIMULUS**
**'MALIBU ORANGE'**
MONKEY-FLOWER
*Semihardy annual*

This tender perennial is usually grown as a semihardy annual for creating a wealth of golden–orange flowers in borders and containers throughout summer. It has both a compact and prostrate nature.

There are many other related varieties, in a color range that includes cream, red, and burgundy.

❋ **HEIGHT** 6–8in (15–20cm)

❋ **SPREAD** 8–12in (20–30cm)

❋ **SITUATION** Full sun or light shade

❋ **SOIL** Moisture-retentive

❋ **HARDINESS** Will not tolerate temperatures below 32°F (0°C)

❋ **ZONES** Hardy annual in zones 2–8 and cool part of zone 9; perennial in warm zone 9 and zones 10–11

**TAGETES PATULA**
**'AURORA'**
FRENCH MARIGOLD
*Semihardy annual*

A well-known marigold with a bushy habit and dark green, deeply cut and divided, fragrant leaves. From early summer to the frosts of fall it creates a wealth of light orange flowers, each about 2in (5cm) wide.

There are many other varieties, in single- and double-flowered forms and in a color range that includes yellow and mahogany red.

❋ **HEIGHT** 8in (20cm)

❋ **SPREAD** 8in (20cm)

❋ **SITUATION** Full sun

❋ **SOIL** Moderately rich and well-drained

❋ **HARDINESS** Will not tolerate temperatures below 32°F (0°C)

❋ **ZONES** Warm-season annual in zones 2–11

**TROPAEOLUM MAJUS**
**'WHIRLYBIRD TANGERINE'**
NASTURTIUM
*Hardy annual*

A spectacular, free-flowering dwarf nasturtium with semidouble, tangerine-colored flowers that are carried well above the foliage. They appear from early summer until early fall.

There are several other varieties in this dwarf series of nasturtiums and they include colors such as cherry rose, cream, gold, mahogany, orange, and scarlet.

- ❋ HEIGHT 1–1¼ft (30–38cm)
- ❋ SPREAD 10–12in (25–30cm)
- ❋ SITUATION Full sun
- ❋ SOIL Moderate fertility and well-drained
- ❋ HARDINESS Tolerates slight frost
- ❋ ZONES Cool-season annual in zones 2–11

**ZINNIA ELEGANS**
**'SHORT STUFF ORANGE'**
COMMON ZINNIA
*Semihardy annual*

A well-known annual with a wealth of mid-green, oval, and pointed leaves borne on stiff and upright stems. From midsummer to early fall it develops petal-packed, daisylike orange flowers.

There are many varieties, in colors including white, purple, orange, yellow, red, and pink, as well as lime-green.

This particular variety is relatively low-growing, but others are taller.

- ❋ HEIGHT 10–15in (25–38cm)
- ❋ SPREAD 10–12in (25–30cm)
- ❋ SITUATION Full sun
- ❋ SOIL Fertile and well-drained
- ❋ HARDINESS Will not tolerate temperatures below 32°F (0°C)
- ❋ ZONES Warm-season annual in zones 2–11

**CROCOSMIA ×**
**CROCOSMIIFLORA**
**'EMILY MACKENZIE'**
MONTBRETIA
*Corm*

A slightly tender cormous plant, with upright, swordlike, mid-green leaves. From midsummer to early fall it bears trumpet-shaped and nodding, dark orange flowers with red splashes in the paler throats, borne on thin, strong stems.

In wet situations dig up the corms in fall and store in a frostproof shed. Replant them 2–3in (5–7.5cm) deep in small groups in spring. In mild areas they can be left outside and covered with leafmold.

☀ HEIGHT 1½–2ft (45–60cm)

☀ SPREAD Space corms 4–6in (10–15cm) apart

☀ SITUATION Warm and sheltered; on the sunny side of a wall

☀ SOIL Light, sandy, and well-drained but moisture-retentive

☀ HARDINESS -10° to -20°F (-23° to -28°C)

☀ ZONES 6–10

**FRITILLARIA IMPERIALIS**
**'AURORA'**
CROWN IMPERIAL
*Bulb*

A spectacular hardy bulb with narrow, glossy-green, lance-shaped leaves clustered in whorls around the lower half of each upright stem. Pendent, tulip-shaped, 2in (5cm) long, orange-yellow flowers cluster around the stem's top during mid- and late spring and smell pungently of garlic.

Other varieties extend the color range to lemon-yellow, red, and orange-brown.

Plant the bulbs 8in (20cm) deep and leave them alone for four or five years.

☀ HEIGHT 2–3ft (60–90cm)

☀ SPREAD Space bulbs 8–12in (20–30cm) apart

☀ SITUATION Full sun

☀ SOIL Fertile and well-drained

☀ HARDINESS -20° to -30°F (-28° to -34°C)

☀ ZONES 5–8

**HYACINTHUS ORIENTALIS
'GYPSY QUEEN'**
COMMON HYACINTH
*Bulb*

A distinctive bulbous plant, with upright, soldierlike spires packed with pale salmon-orange, bell-shaped flowers during late spring.

These bulbs are planted 5–6in (13–15cm) deep in early fall to create color in spring-flowering displays. After flowering, the bulbs should be dug up so that summer-flowering plants can be put in their place.

Other varieties extend the color range to white, yellow, red, pink, and blue.

※ HEIGHT 6–9in (15–23cm)
※ SPREAD Space bulbs 6–8in (15–20cm) apart
※ SITUATION Full sun
※ SOIL Moderately fertile, moisture-retentive but well-drained
※ HARDINESS 20° to 10°F. (-6° to -12°C)
※ ZONES 3–7

**LILIUM
'ENCHANTMENT'**
LILY
*Bulb*

A Mid-Century Hybrid, with upward- and outward-facing, cup-shaped, orange-red flowers with black spots during early summer. Each flower is up to 6in (15cm) across.

As well as being grown in a border, it can be planted in pots on a patio. Additionally, it is ideal as a cut-flower for room decoration.

Plant these bulbs 4–6in (10–15cm) deep.

※ HEIGHT 2–3ft (60–90cm)
※ SPREAD Space bulbs 9in (23cm) apart
※ SITUATION Full sun or partial shade
※ SOIL Well-drained
※ HARDINESS 0° to -10°F (-17° to -23°C)
※ ZONES 4–8

## TULIPA
### 'ORANJE NASSAU'
TULIP
*Bulb*

A double-early tulip, with large, double-flowered orange flowers during late spring. Each flower is 3–4in (7.5–10cm) across.

It is ideal for planting in late summer or early fall for blooming in spring-flowering bedding displays. Plant the bulbs 5–6in (13–15cm) deep in most soils, but slightly deeper in sandy soil types.

After flowering, the bulbs should be lifted and summer-flowering plants put in their place.

* HEIGHT 1–1¼ft (30–38cm)
* SPREAD Space bulbs 5–6in (13–15cm) apart
* SITUATION Full sun
* SOIL Well-drained but moisture-retentive and slightly alkaline
* HARDINESS -20° to -30°F (-28° to -34°C)
* ZONES 4–7; zones 8–11 use as an annual

## ALSTROEMERIA AUREA
### 'DOVER ORANGE'
### ALSTROEMERIA AURANTIACA
### 'DOVER ORANGE'
YELLOW ALSTROEMERIA
*Herbaceous perennial*

A fleshy, tuberous-rooted border plant with an upright, clump-forming nature. It bears deep orange, irregularly trumpet-shaped flowers from early to late summer.

Other varieties include white, yellow, lilac, pink, and scarlet.

Plant the fleshy tubers 4–6in (10–15cm) deep.

* HEIGHT 3ft (90cm)
* SPREAD 1–1¼ft (30–38cm)
* SITUATION Full sun; shelter
* SOIL Fertile and well-drained
* HARDINESS 10° to 0°F (-12° to -17°C)
* ZONES 7–10

ALSTROEMERIA AUREA 'DOVER ORANGE'

**ASCLEPIAS TUBEROSA**
BUTTERFLY MILKWEED
*Herbaceous perennial*

A tuberous-rooted, woody-based perennial with an upright nature and narrowly lance-shaped, mid-green leaves. The small, scented, bright orange flowers are borne in broad, crownlike heads during mid- and late summer.

This is often a difficult plant to establish and, once growing strongly, is best left alone.

There are several varieties, with colors encompassing orange, red, pink, and gold.

※ HEIGHT 1½–2½ft (45–75cm)
※ SPREAD Space 9–12in
  (23–30cm) apart
※ SITUATION Full sun and shelter, preferably close to a warm wall
※ SOIL Deeply cultivated, light, and moisture-retentive
※ HARDINESS -30° to -40°F
  (-34° to -40°C)
※ ZONES 4–9

**CHRYSANTHEMUM 'APRICOT'**
DENDRANTHEMA 'APRICOT'
*Herbaceous perennial*

This well-known chrysanthemum, partly derived from *Chrysanthemum rubellum*, creates masses of 1½–2in (36–50mm) wide, single, apricot-colored flowers with yellow centers. They drench borders with color from late summer to mid-fall and have a clump-forming nature.

There are many other varieties, in colors that mainly include yellow, pink, red, and crimson.

※ HEIGHT 2½–3ft (75–90cm)
※ SPREAD 1½ft (45cm)
※ SITUATION Full sun
※ SOIL Fertile, slightly alkaline, and moisture-retentive but well-drained
※ HARDINESS -10° to -20°F
  (-23° to -28°C)
※ ZONES 4–9

## EUPHORBIA GRIFFITHII 'FIREGLOW'
*Rhizomatous perennial*

A magnificent, upright, and bushy border plant with mid-green, lance-shaped leaves with pink midribs. During late spring and early summer brilliant, flame-colored bracts appear in rounded clusters, up to 4in (10cm) across.

- HEIGHT 2–2½ft (60–75cm)
- SPREAD 1½ft (45cm)
- SITUATION Full sun or light shade
- SOIL Well-drained
- HARDINESS -10° to -20°F (-23° to -28°C)
- ZONES 4–8

## GEUM 'BORISII'
GEUM × BORISII
BORIS AVENS
*Herbaceous perennial*

A long-lived and reliable border plant, with mid-green leaves. Orange-scarlet, bowl-shaped flowers, each about 1in (2.5cm) across, are borne on branching stems mainly during late spring and early summer, and often intermittently throughout the summer as well.

Other geums have flowers in yellow, deep pink, and scarlet.

- HEIGHT 1ft (30cm)
- SPREAD 10–12in (25–30cm)
- SITUATION Full sun or partial shade
- SOIL Well-drained but moisture-retentive
- HARDINESS -20° to -30°F (-28° to -34°C)
- ZONES 5–7

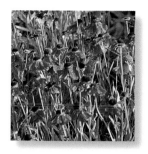

**HELENIUM
'MOERHEIM BEAUTY'**
HELENIUM FALLALE
'MOERHEIM BEAUTY'
SNEEZEWEED
*Herbaceous perennial*

**KNIPHOFIA
'ALCAZAR'**
TORCH-LILY
*Herbaceous perennial*

A clump-forming border plant with upright stems packed with mid-green, lance-shaped leaves. From midsummer to early fall it creates a mass of large, daisylike, bronze-red flowers, each with a large, dominant central disc.

There are several other varieties, in colors that include yellow, golden-orange, copper-red, red, and golden-brown.

A distinctive border plant, with narrow, rushlike, mid-green leaves and tall stems bearing pokerlike heads of orange flowers during early and midsummer.

There are many other varieties, extending the color range to ivory white, yellow, lemon, bright scarlet, and red.

☀ HEIGHT 3ft (90cm)
☀ SPREAD 1–1½ft (30–45cm)
☀ SITUATION Full sun
☀ SOIL Well-drained but moisture-retentive
☀ HARDINESS -30° to -40°F
  (-34° to -40°C)
☀ ZONES 3–8

☀ HEIGHT 3ft (90cm)
☀ SPREAD 1½ft (45cm)
☀ SITUATION Full sun
☀ SOIL Well-drained
☀ HARDINESS 20° to 10°F
  (-6° to -12°C)
☀ ZONES 5–9

## BERBERIS LINEARIFOLIA
## 'ORANGE KING'
BARBERRY
*Evergreen shrub*

With an upright and slow-growing nature, this shrub is ideal for small gardens where it reveals glossy, deep green, narrow leaves and clusters of rich orange and apricot flowers in mid- and late spring. These are followed by round, black berries, which have a waxy, blue-white bloom to them.

- ❄ HEIGHT 6–10ft (1.8–3m)
- ❄ SPREAD 3–4ft (90cm–1.2m)
- ❄ SITUATION A warm, sheltered position against a sunny wall
- ❄ SOIL Well-drained
- ❄ HARDINESS 0° to -10°F (-17° to -23°C)
- ❄ ZONES 5–8

## HELIANTHEMUM
## NUMMULARIUM
## 'FIRE DRAGON'
COMMON SUNROSE
*Evergreen shrub*

With a low and slightly sprawling nature, this shrub is ideal for trailing over the edges of raised beds or covering soil alongside paths. During early and midsummer, the narrow, glossy, deep green leaves are surmounted by masses of cup-shaped, flame-orange flowers, each with a yellow center.

There are many varieties, in a color range that includes yellow, rose-pink, and rosy red, as well as bicolored varieties.

- ❄ HEIGHT 4–6in (10–15cm)
- ❄ SPREAD 1½–2ft (45–60cm)
- ❄ SITUATION Full sun
- ❄ SOIL Well-drained
- ❄ HARDINESS -10° to -20°F (-23° to -28°C)
- ❄ ZONES 6–9

**PHYGELIUS × RECTUS**
**'AFRICAN QUEEN'**
**PHYGELIUS × RECTUS**
**'INDIAN CHIEF'**
CAPE-FUCHSIA
*Evergreen shrub*

**POTENTILLA FRUTICOSA**
**'TANGERINE'**
BUSH CINQUEFOIL
*Deciduous shrub*

A tender, clump-forming border shrub with upright stems bearing tooth-edged, lance-shaped, mid-green leaves and orange-red flowers borne in lax clusters up to 9in (23cm) long, from midsummer to early or mid-fall.

In cold areas it is usually treated as an herbaceous perennial, with the stems being cut back to ground level in early spring.

There are several other varieties, in colors including pale red, orange-red, deep red-pink, orange, and yellow.

A bushy but compact shrub with small, mid-green leaves and masses of tangerine-orange flowers that become bright yellow in full sun. Each flower is about 1in (2.5cm) across, and they appear from early to late summer. Sometimes flowering extends into the early fall.

Other shrubby potentillas have attractive flowers, in many shades of yellow and red.

☀ HEIGHT 2–2½ft (60–75cm)
☀ SPREAD 1½–2ft (45–60cm)
☀ SITUATION Full sun and shelter
☀ SOIL Light and well-drained
☀ HARDINESS 20° to 10°F
  (-6° to -12°C)
☀ ZONES 8–10

☀ HEIGHT 2ft (60cm)
☀ SPREAD 3¼–4ft (1–1.2m)
☀ SITUATION Full sun
☀ SOIL Light, and well-drained but moisture-retentive
☀ HARDINESS 10° to 0°F
  (-12° to -17°C)
☀ ZONES 2–7

**RHODODENDRON
'GIBRALTAR'**
*Deciduous shrub*

A popular Knap Hill Hybrid
bearing trumpet-shaped, flame-
orange flowers with crinkly petals.
They are borne in large trusses
during late spring. The buds are an
attractive deep orange–crimson.

☀ HEIGHT 6–8ft (1.8–2.4m)

☀ SPREAD 5–7ft (1.5–2.1m)

☀ SITUATION Dappled light or partial
shade, with shelter from cold, strong,
drying wind

☀ SOIL Slightly acid, and moisture-
retentive but well-drained

☀ HARDINESS 20° to 10°F
(-6° to -12°C)

☀ ZONES 5–8

**ROSA FOETIDA
'BICOLOR'**
AUSTRIAN COPPER BRIER
*Deciduous shrub*

A spreading and suckering shrub
with arching, dark brown stems and
single flowers during late spring
and into early summer. They are a
vivid nasturtium-orange on the
upper side, and yellow on the
reverse. Each flower is 2–2½in
(5–6.5cm) wide.

☀ HEIGHT 4–5ft (1.2–1.5m)

☀ SPREAD 4–5ft (1.2–1.5m)

☀ SITUATION Full sun

☀ SOIL Fertile, and moisture-retentive
but well-drained

☀ HARDINESS -20° to -30°F
(-28° to -34°C)

☀ ZONES 4–8

## CAMPSIS GRANDIFLORA
CHINESE TRUMPET VINE
*Deciduous climbing shrub*

A spectacular, slightly tender climber, with a vigorous and branching habit and mid-green leaves formed of seven or nine leaflets. During late summer and early fall it bears deep orange and red, trumpet-shaped flowers in terminal clusters. Each flower is about 2–3in (5–7.5cm) long.

It is self-clinging and quickly secures itself to a trellis. A warm, sheltered position is essential.

※ HEIGHT Up to 30ft (9m)
※ SPREAD Up to 15ft (4.5m)
※ SITUATION Full sun and shelter from cold wind
※ SOIL Fertile and well-drained; dig plenty of well-decayed compost or farmyard manure into the soil
※ HARDINESS 20° to 10°F (-6° to -12°C)
※ ZONES 7–9

## ECCREMOCARPUS SCABER
CHILEAN GLORYFLOWER
*Evergreen climber*

A vigorous, fast-growing, semi-woody climber, with dark green leaves formed of many leaflets. From early summer to early fall it bears nodding, tubular, orange-scarlet flowers in clusters of ten to twelve.

It climbs by means of tendrils and is ideal for covering an arch or pergola, or a wall with a trellis secured to it.

※ HEIGHT 8–10ft (2.4–3m)
※ SPREAD 6–8ft (1.8–2.4m)
※ SITUATION Sunny and wind-sheltered
※ SOIL Fertile, and moisture-retentive but well-drained
※ HARDINESS 30° to 20°F (-1° to -6°C)
※ ZONES Tender, warm-season annual in zones 4–11

**EUONYMUS EUROPAEUS**
COMMON SPINDLE TREE
*Deciduous shrub or small tree*

With a spreading and bushy habit, and often bare of leaves toward its base, this shrub bears slender-pointed, mid-green leaves. The green and white flowers are inconspicuous and borne in late spring, but they are followed by rose-red capsules, which open to reveal orange seeds.

No regular pruning is needed, other than occasionally thinning out shoots in late winter.

※ HEIGHT 6–10ft (1.8–3m)
※ SPREAD 5–8ft (1.5–2.4m)
※ SITUATION Sun or partial shade
※ SOIL Well-drained
※ HARDINESS -30° to -40°F
    (-34° to -40°C)
※ ZONES 3–7

**HIPPOPHAE RHAMNOIDES**
COMMON SEA BUCKTHORN
*Deciduous shrub*

Bushy and sometimes with a tree-like stature, its branches are covered with sharp spines and narrow, silvery leaves. Inconspicuous yellow flowers appear in mid- and late spring. In fall and winter only female plants bear the small, round, bright orange berries, but both male and female plants are required to be present in order to produce these. The berries are disliked by birds and therefore persist throughout much of the winter.

No regular pruning is needed, but cut out straggly or dead shoots in midsummer.

※ HEIGHT 8–10ft (2.4–3m)
※ SPREAD 8–10ft (2.4–3m)
※ SITUATION Full sun or partial shade;
    it grows well in coastal areas
※ SOIL Well-drained
※ HARDINESS -30° to -40°F
    (-34° to -40°C)
※ ZONES 3–7

**PHYSALIS ALKEKENGI**
CHINESE-LANTERN
*Herbaceous perennial*

A clump-forming and spreading
plant with upright, unbranched
stems bearing light to mid-green
leaves and ⅛in (2.5cm) wide white
flowers during mid- and late
summer. These are following by
bright red calyces about 2in (5cm)
long; each one encloses an orange-
red berry.

- ☀ HEIGHT 1–1¼ft (30–38cm)
- ☀ SPREAD 1½ft (45cm)
- ☀ SITUATION Full sun
- ☀ SOIL Well-drained
- ☀ HARDINESS 0° to -10°F
  (-17° to -23°C)
- ☀ ZONES 5–7

**PYRACANTHA
'ORANGE CHARMER'**
FIRETHORN
*Evergreen shrub*

With an upright nature, this shrub
is ideal for planting against a wall.
The stems are spiny and the bright
orange-red fruits appear during
early fall and persist right
into winter.

There are many related species
with colored berries, usually in
yellow, orange-red, and bright red.

- ☀ HEIGHT 8–10ft (2.4–3m)
- ☀ SPREAD 5–6ft (1.5–1.8m)
- ☀ SITUATION Full sun or partial shade
- ☀ SOIL Fertile and well-drained
- ☀ HARDINESS 20° to 10°F
  (-6° to -12°C)
- ☀ ZONES 6–9

## AMELANCHIER LAMARCKII
SNOWY SERVICEBERRY
*Deciduous shrub or small tree*

An outstandingly beautiful shrub or small tree, with a wealth of pure white, star-shaped flowers during spring. In fall the mid-green leaves assume rich tints of red and soft yellow.

No regular pruning is needed.

☀ HEIGHT 15–25ft (4.5–7.5m)

☀ SPREAD 12–20ft (3.6–6m)

☀ SITUATION Full sun or light shade

☀ SOIL Lime-free, moisture-retentive, but well-drained; the soil should not dry out during summer

☀ HARDINESS -20° to -30°F (-28° to -34°C)

☀ ZONES 4–8

## ARONIA MELANOCARPA
BLACK CHOKEBERRY
*Deciduous shrub*

A bushy, somewhat flat-topped shrub with a suckering nature. The shiny, dark green, and pear-shaped leaves assume rich shades of brownish-red in fall.

During late spring it develops white, hawthornlike flowers, which are followed in fall by lustrous black fruits.

No regular pruning is needed, other than thinning out shoots in spring.

☀ HEIGHT 3–5ft (90cm–1.5m)

☀ SPREAD 4–6ft (1.2–1.8m)

☀ SITUATION Full sun or light shade

☀ SOIL Well-drained, but moisture-retentive and slightly acid; it will not grow in shallow, chalky soil

☀ HARDINESS -20° to -30°F (-28° to -34°C)

☀ ZONES 3–8

**CORNUS FLORIDA**
FLOWERING DOGWOOD
*Deciduous shrub or small tree*

Spreading and well-branched, this plant has dark green leaves, which in fall turn brilliant shades of orange and scarlet. In late spring and early summer it produces green flowers surrounded by large, white, petal-like bracts.

No regular pruning is needed.

- ☀ HEIGHT 10–15ft (3–4.5m)
- ☀ SPREAD 10–18ft (3–5.4m)
- ☀ SITUATION Full sun or partial shade
- ☀ SOIL Light, neutral, or slightly acid, and well-drained but moisture-retentive
- ☀ HARDINESS -10° to -20°F (-23° to -28°C)
- ☀ ZONES 5–9

**COTINUS COGGYGRIA**
**RHUS COTINUS**
SMOKE TREE
*Deciduous shrub*

A bushy, rounded shrub, with round to pear-shaped, light green leaves that assume rich colors in fall. Additionally, during midsummer it reveals lax and feathery clusters, 6–8in (15–20cm) long, of small purple flowers. These create the impression of smoke, hence its common name.

No regular pruning is needed, other than cutting out dead and straggly growth in early spring.

- ☀ HEIGHT 6–8ft (1.8–2.4m)
- ☀ SPREAD 6–8ft (1.8–2.4m)
- ☀ SITUATION Full sun
- ☀ SOIL Well-drained
- ☀ HARDINESS -10° to -20°F (-23° to -28°C)
- ☀ ZONES 4–8

## DISANTHUS CERCIDIFOLIUS
*Deciduous shrub*

A rounded, bushy, and upright shrub with heart-shaped to rounded leaves that reveal a blue-green cast. In fall they assume rich scarlet and red shades.

No regular pruning is needed, other than cutting out straggly shoots in late winter.

- ☀ HEIGHT 6–10ft (1.8–3m)
- ☀ SPREAD 7–8ft (2.1–2.4m)
- ☀ SITUATION Full sun or partial shade
- ☀ SOIL Neutral or slightly acid, and moisture-retentive but well-drained
- ☀ HARDINESS 20° to 10°F (-6° to -12°C)
- ☀ ZONES 5–8

## ENKIANTHUS CAMPANULATUS
*Deciduous shrub*

An upright and bushy shrub with dull green, finely tooth-edged leaves that turn brilliant red in fall. Additionally, it bears masses of small, bell-shaped, creamy yellow flowers with red veins during late spring and early summer.

No regular pruning is needed.

- ☀ HEIGHT 6–8ft (1.8–2.4m)
- ☀ SPREAD 4–6ft (1.2–1.8m)
- ☀ SITUATION Light, dappled shade
- ☀ SOIL Slightly acid or neutral, moisture-retentive, and enriched with peat and leafmold
- ☀ HARDINESS -10° to -20°F (-23° to -28°C)
- ☀ ZONES 4–7

**EUONYMUS ALATUS**
WINGED EUONYMUS
*Deciduous shrub*

With a stiff and open habit, this slow-growing shrub displays oval to pear-shaped, dark green leaves, which in fall turn light scarlet and red. Small, greenish-yellow flowers appear in late spring and early summer and are followed by purple fruits.

No regular pruning is needed, other than cutting out straggly shoots in late winter.

❉ HEIGHT 6–8ft (1.8–2.4m)

❉ SPREAD 6–8ft (1.8–2.4m)

❉ SITUATION Full sun or partial shade

❉ SOIL Well-drained

❉ HARDINESS -30° to -40°F (-34° to -40°C)

❉ ZONES 4–8

**FOTHERGILLA MAJOR**
*Deciduous shrub*

A slow-growing shrub with white, sweetly scented, bottlebrush-like flowers in clusters up to 2in (5cm) long during late spring. In fall the dark green leaves assume rich red and orange-yellow tints.

No regular pruning is needed, other than occasionally cutting out misplaced or damaged shoots during spring.

❉ HEIGHT 6–8ft (1.8–2.4m)

❉ SPREAD 4–6ft (1.2–1.8m)

❉ SITUATION Full sun

❉ SOIL Fertile, slightly acid, and moisture-retentive

❉ HARDINESS -10° to -20°F (-23° to -28°C)

❉ ZONES 4–8

**NANDINA DOMESTICA**
*Semihardy evergreen shrub*

Although claimed to resemble a
bamboo, this has a different nature
and is a slightly tender evergreen
shrub. In cold winters shoots and
leaves are often damaged, but plants
usually recover.

It has pale to mid–green leaves,
each formed of many leaflets,
which in mid- and late fall assume
red and purple shades.

During midsummer it bears white
flowers in large, lax heads. These
are followed in fall by white or
scarlet fruits.

☀ **HEIGHT** 4–7ft (1.2–2.1m)

☀ **SPREAD** 2–3ft (60–90cm)

☀ **SITUATION** Sunny and sheltered
from cold wind

☀ **SOIL** Fertile, and moisture-retentive
but well-drained

☀ **HARDINESS** 10° to 0°F
(-12° to -17°C)

☀ **ZONES** 6–9

**PARTHENOCISSUS
QUINQUEFOLIA**
**VITIS QUINQUEFOLIA**
VIRGINIA CREEPER
*Deciduous climber*

A vigorous climber with dull
green, five-lobed leaves, which in
fall assume brilliant orange and
scarlet shades.

It has tendrils and is therefore
self-clinging on walls and fences, as
well as scaling large pergolas. It will
also climb rough-barked trees.

☀ **HEIGHT** 35–60ft (10.5–18m) or more

☀ **SPREAD** 20ft (6m) or more

☀ **SITUATION** Full sun or light shade

☀ **SOIL** Fertile, and well-drained but
moisture-retentive

☀ **HARDINESS** -30° to -40°F
(-34° to -40°C)

☀ **ZONES** 3–9

**RHUS TYPHINA**
STAGHORN SUMACH
*Deciduous shrub*

A distinctive shrub, with large, mid-green leaves, often 1½ft (45cm) long and formed of 13–26 leaflets. In fall they assume rich shades of orange, red, and purple. The stems are densely covered with reddish hairs.

The form 'Laciniata' has finely cut leaves, but does not assume such rich colors in fall.

No regular pruning is needed.

❋ HEIGHT 8–12ft (2.4–3.6m)
❋ SPREAD 8–12ft (2.4–3.6m)
❋ SITUATION Full sun
❋ SOIL Well-drained
❋ HARDINESS -30° to -40°F (-34° to -40°C)
❋ ZONES 3–8

**VITIS COIGNETIAE**
GLORYVINE
*Deciduous climber*

A vigorous, spectacular vine with large, rounded but lobed, mid-green leaves; their undersides are attractively covered in rust-red hairs. In fall the leaves assume rich colors, first yellow, then orange-red, and eventually crimson.

It clings to supports and is best used to clothe very large pergolas, or to scramble into trees.

❋ HEIGHT 40ft (12m) or more
❋ SPREAD 20ft (6m) or more
❋ SITUATION Full sun or light shade
❋ SOIL Fertile, and well-drained but moisture-retentive; it does not like acid soil
❋ HARDINESS -10° to -20°F (-23° to -28°C)
❋ ZONES 4–9

*Orange and red harmonize naturally in fall colors.*

# index for orange

*See the following pages for other plants with several varieties, including orange:*

CALENDULA OFFICINALIS

# RED

Red is usually associated with
summer, and with beds of red roses
sizzling in the heat, but can be used
all year round.

# the color red
# red plants

*There are so many different reds to be found in flowers— the scarlet of this Geum is just one example.*

Red is one of our loveliest colors in the garden but, at the same time, is perhaps the most difficult. There is such a wide range of very different reds, from vivid scarlets (as in *Pelargonium × Hortorum* 'Multibloom Scarlet'), which are on the orange side of the red divide, through the true red of *Lobelia cardinalis* to the deeper velvet-red of *Rosa* 'Josephine Bruce'. There is also a wide range of red fruits, from the scarlet, goblet-shaped hips of *Rosa moyesii* to the bunches of sealing-wax-red berries of *Ilex verticillata* and the wonderful rich red of the eating apple Worcester Pearmain. Truly red leaves are rare and do not merit a separate entry in the plant directory, but there is a startling red-leaved grass— *Imperata cylindrica* 'Rubra'—which is worth including in any red planting scheme. Red stems are found in several of the dogwoods: the brightest color being found in *Cornus alba* 'Westonbirt', with a more orange-red in the willow *Salix alba* 'Chermesina' and a dark plum-red in the stems of *Cornus alba* 'Kesselringii'.

## COLOR HARMONIES

Red is adjacent to orange and purple, and opposite green, in the spectrum, so a variety of potential color schemes is possible. The scarlets mix most comfortably with orange, as seen in so many leaves as they color up in fall. Similar color mixtures are found in

SALVIA SPLENDENS

*A dark red border consisting of both flowers and foliage stands out particularly well against the surrounding greens of plants and stems.*

nasturtiums, dahlias, chrysanthemums, and tuberous begonias. In association with purple, use the deeper reds and reds with a hint of blue—for ideas look at the wide range of red-purple color combinations found in fuchsias. Green and red comprises a classic pair of opposite and complementary colors and is best seen when the reds are restricted to pure red, as in a bed of *Rosa* 'Trumpeter' set against a background of green leaves; or, in a damper area, a planting of *Lobelia cardinalis* among a group of hosta.

## USING RED IN YOUR GARDEN

Red can be used as a garden color all year round, with beds of red tulips in spring and red flowers against plum foliage in the fall. It is particularly valuable in winter, when holly berries indicate that it is nearly Christmas and brighten up the dreariest of days.

### DIANTHUS BARBATUS
SWEET WILLIAM
*Biennial*

Sweet Williams are well-known perennials traditionally raised and grown as hardy biennials for flowering during early and mid-summer. Some varieties, however, are better grown as hardy annuals and sown in borders in spring, where they flower a few months later. Sweet Williams have a relaxed, cottage-garden nature and are available in a wide color range, including red, crimson, salmon-pink, and pink.

- ☀ **HEIGHT** 6–10in (15–25cm)
- ☀ **SPREAD** 6–8in (15–20cm)
- ☀ **SITUATION** Full sun
- ☀ **SOIL** Well-drained; apply lime if the soil is acid
- ☀ **HARDINESS** Tolerates temperatures down to about 20°F (-6°C)
- ☀ **ZONES** Hardy cool-season biennial in zones 3–9

### ERYSIMUM CHEIRI 'BLOOD RED'
CHEIRANTHUS CHEIRI 'BLOOD RED'
WALLFLOWER
*Biennial*

This well-known hardy perennial is invariably grown as a hardy biennial for flowering during late spring and early summer. The range of varieties is wide, but 'Blood Red' develops fragrant, deep velvety, blood-red flowers.

- ☀ **HEIGHT** 1–1¼ft (30–38cm)
- ☀ **SPREAD** 8–10in (20–25cm)
- ☀ **SITUATION** Full sun
- ☀ **SOIL** Fertile, well-drained, and slightly alkaline
- ☀ **HARDINESS** Tolerates temperatures down to about 20°F (-6°C)
- ☀ **ZONES** Biennial, grown as an annual in cold winter zones

## PELARGONIUM × HORTORUM 'MULTIBLOOM SCARLET'
COMMON GERANIUM
*Semihardy annual*

This glorious tender perennial is invariably grown as a semihardy annual. There is a wide range of separate colors, including scarlet, pink, salmon, bright rose, and white.

❋ HEIGHT 1–1¼ft (30–38cm)

❋ SPREAD 10–12in (25–30cm)

❋ SITUATION Full sun

❋ SOIL Light, and moisture-retentive but well-drained

❋ HARDINESS Will not tolerate temperatures below 32°F (0°C)

❋ ZONES Tender perennial, grown as an annual in zones 2–9; overwinters in zones 10–11

## PRIMULA × POLYANTHA
POLYANTHUS
*Hardy biennial*

Often listed as a Pruhonicensis Hybrid, this polyanthus floods gardens with color in spring. It derives from four main primulas: *P. vulgaris* (English primrose), *P. veris* (cowslip primrose), *P. elatior* (oxlip primrose) and *P. juliae* (Julia primrose). It is also sometimes listed as *Primula variabilis*. There are several strains, in colors including blue, cream, yellow, white, pink, red, crimson, and scarlet.

It is usually raised as a hardy biennial, but can also be grown as a perennial or semihardy annual.

❋ HEIGHT 8–12in (20–30cm)

❋ SPREAD 8–10in (20–25cm)

❋ SITUATION Full sun or partial shade

❋ SOIL Fertile, and well-drained but moisture-retentive

❋ HARDINESS Will not tolerate temperatures below 32°F (0°C)

❋ ZONES 3–8

## SALVIA SPLENDENS
SCARLET SAGE
*Semihardy annual*

This dramatic bedding plant is a semihardy perennial invariably grown as a semihardy annual. It develops bright green leaves, with scarlet flowers borne in broad spikes from midsummer to fall.

There are several varieties in other colors, including purple, salmon, and white.

❋ HEIGHT 1–1¼ft (30–38cm)
❋ SPREAD 1–1¼ft (30–38cm)
❋ SITUATION Full sun
❋ SOIL Light and well-drained
❋ HARDINESS Will not tolerate temperatures below 32°F (0°C)
❋ ZONES Semi-hardy summer annual in zones 2–10; spring or fall annual in zones 10–11

## TAGETES
'DISCO RED'
TAGETES PATULA 'DISCO RED'
FRENCH MARIGOLD
*Semihardy annual*

This spectacular semihardy annual creates a riot of richly red flowers from early summer until the frosts of fall. These are borne amid dark green, scented, deeply cut and divided leaves.

There are many other French marigolds, in single- and double-flowered forms and mainly in red, brownish-crimson, orange, and yellow shades.

❋ HEIGHT 8–10in (20–25cm)
❋ SPREAD 8–10in (20–25cm)
❋ SITUATION Full sun
❋ SOIL Moderately rich and well-drained
❋ HARDINESS Will not tolerate temperatures below 32°F (0°C)
❋ ZONES Warm-season annual in zones 2–11

SALVIA SPLENDENS

## ANEMONE CORONARIA
### 'HOLLANDIA'
#### ANEMONE CORONARIA
### 'HIS EXCELLENCY'
POPPY ANEMONE
*Corm*

This De Caen–type anemone creates a wealth of single, scarlet flowers, each up to 2in (5cm) wide, during late spring. Each plant produces up to 20 flowers, which are borne among light to mid-green, feathery leaves.

Other varieties of these superb cormous plants have white, blue, and red flowers.

Plant the corms 1½–2in (36–50mm) deep in early fall.

☀ HEIGHT 6–10in (15–25cm)

☀ SPREAD Space corms 6in (15cm) apart

☀ SITUATION Full sun or light shade

☀ SOIL Well-drained

☀ HARDINESS 20° to 10°F (-6° to -12°C)

☀ ZONES 3–11

## TULIPA PRAESTANS
### 'FUSILIER'
LEATHER-BULB TULIP
*Bulb*

This species tulip has broad, gray-green leaves and stems that bear two to five red flowers, each about 2in (5cm) long, during mid- and late spring.

There are many other varieties, all in shades of red.

Plant the bulbs in fall, setting them 5–6in (13–15cm) deep in most soils, but slightly deeper in light, sandy types.

☀ HEIGHT 1–1½ft (30–45cm)

☀ SPREAD Space bulbs 5–6in (13–15cm) apart

☀ SITUATION Full sun and shelter from strong, cold wind

☀ SOIL Well-drained but moisture-retentive, and slightly alkaline

☀ HARDINESS -10° to -20°F (-23° to -28°C)

☀ ZONES 4–7

## ACHILLEA 'FANAL'
### ACHILLEA MILLEFOLIUM 'THE BEACON'
YARROW
*Herbaceous perennial*

A sturdy, clump-forming border plant with dark green, feathery, pungent leaves and flattened heads, about 4in (10cm) wide, packed with crimson-red flowers from early to late summer.

There are several other superb varieties, in colors from white to cerise.

❋ HEIGHT 2–2½ft (60–75cm)

❋ SPREAD 15in (38cm)

❋ SITUATION Full sun

❋ SOIL Well-drained

❋ HARDINESS -40° to -50°F (-40° to -45°C)

❋ ZONES 3–9

## COSMOS ATROSANGUINEUS
### BIDENS ATROSANGUINEA
CHOCOLATE COSMOS
*Herbaceous perennial*

A somewhat straggly border plant with velvety maroon, chocolate-scented flowers, each about 1⅜in (36mm) wide, from early summer to early fall. The flowers are borne amid finely cut, deep green leaves.

❋ HEIGHT 2–2½ft (60–75cm)

❋ SPREAD 1½–1¾ft (45–50cm)

❋ SITUATION Full sun

❋ SOIL Light, and well-drained but moisture-retentive

❋ HARDINESS 20° to 10°F (-6° to -12°C)

❋ ZONES Grow as an annual in zones 2–11

## GEUM
### 'MRS. J. BRADSHAW'
**GEUM CHILOENSE**
**'MRS. BRADSHAW'**
CHILEAN AVENS
*Herbaceous perennial*

A rather sprawling, ground-covering, and long-lived border plant with mid-green leaves and semidouble scarlet flowers borne on branching stems from early to late summer, and often into early fall. Each flower is about 1in (2.5cm) wide.

Other geums have yellow or orange flowers.

☀ HEIGHT 1½–1¾ft (45–50cm)
☀ SPREAD 1–1½ft (30–45cm)
☀ SITUATION Full sun or partial shade
☀ SOIL Well-drained but moisture-retentive, and enriched with garden compost
☀ HARDINESS -10° to -20°F (-23° to -28°C)
☀ ZONES 5–7

## HEUCHERA
### 'RED SPANGLES'
**HEUCHERA SANGUINEA**
**'RED SPANGLES'**
CORAL-BELLS
*Herbaceous perennial*

A distinctive border plant with evergreen, heart-shaped leaves and upright, branching stems bearing tiny, blood-red, bell-shaped flowers from early summer through to early fall.

Other heucheras have flowers in white, pink, and salmon-scarlet.

☀ HEIGHT 1–1½ft (30–45cm)
☀ SPREAD 1¼–1½ft (38–45cm)
☀ SITUATION Full sun or partial shade
☀ SOIL Well-drained but moisture-retentive
☀ HARDINESS -30° to -40°F (-34° to -40°C)
☀ ZONES 4–8

## LOBELIA CARDINALIS
CARDINAL-FLOWER
*Herbaceous perennial*

A color-blazing, short-lived, herbaceous perennial with upright and branched stems bearing mid-green, lance-shaped leaves and clustered spires of scarlet flowers during mid- and late summer.

In cold areas, cover the plants with straw, bracken, or peat in winter to provide protection from the frost.

- ❋ HEIGHT 2–2½ft (60–75cm)
- ❋ SPREAD 1ft (30cm)
- ❋ SITUATION Partial shade and shelter from cold, strong wind
- ❋ SOIL Fertile and moisture-retentive
- ❋ HARDINESS -30° to -40°F (-34° to -40°C)
- ❋ ZONES 2–9

## MONARDA 'CAMBRIDGE SCARLET'
MONARDA DIDYMA
'CAMBRIDGE SCARLET'
BEE-BALM
*Herbaceous perennial*

A bushy and clump-forming border plant with upright stems bearing fragrant, oval to lance-shaped, mid-green, and hairy leaves. From early summer to early fall it bears whorls of hooded, tubular, bright scarlet flowers.

Other varieties extend the color range to white, pink, violet–purple, and soft lavender.

- ❋ HEIGHT 2–2½ft (60–75cm)
- ❋ SPREAD 1¼–1½ft (38–45cm)
- ❋ SITUATION Full sun or partial shade
- ❋ SOIL Fertile and moisture-retentive
- ❋ HARDINESS -20° to -30°F (-28° to -34°C)
- ❋ ZONES 4–9

**PAPAVER ORIENTALE**
'ALLEGRO'
ORIENTAL POPPY
*Herbaceous perennial*

A dominant, clump-forming border plant with large, deeply cut, mid- to deep green, coarse, and hairy leaves. During early summer it develops flamboyant red flowers, each up to 4in (10cm) wide, on long, stiff, and wiry stems.

There are other varieties in a range of colors, including white, pink, and scarlet.

❋ HEIGHT 2–3ft (60–90cm)
❋ SPREAD 1¾–2ft (50–60cm)
❋ SITUATION Full sun
❋ SOIL Well-drained
❋ HARDINESS -30° to -40°F
(-34° to -40°C)
❋ ZONES 2–7

**POTENTILLA**
'GIBSON'S SCARLET'
CINQUEFOIL
*Herbaceous perennial*

A sprawling border plant with an irregular nature and strawberrylike leaves. From early summer to fall it bears semidouble, saucer-shaped, bright-red flowers.

Other varieties extend the color range to yellow, scarlet, crimson-maroon, and orange.

❋ HEIGHT 1ft (30cm)
❋ SPREAD 1¼–1½ft (38–45cm)
❋ SITUATION Full sun
❋ SOIL Well-drained but moisture-retentive
❋ HARDINESS -10° to -20°F
(-23° to -28°C)
❋ ZONES 5–8

## CHAENOMELES × SUPERBA 'CRIMSON AND GOLD'
JAPANESE QUINCE
*Deciduous shrub*

A dense, straggly, and spreading shrub with spiny branches and glossy green leaves. During spring it produces a wealth of flowers with red petals and golden stamens.

There are several other superb varieties, with flower colors that range from pink to crimson.

- ❊ HEIGHT 3ft (90cm)
- ❊ SPREAD 4–5ft (1.2–1.5m)
- ❊ SITUATION Full sun
- ❊ SOIL Well-drained
- ❊ HARDINESS -10° to -20°F (-23° to -28°C)
- ❊ ZONES 4–8

## CRINODENDRON HOOKERIANUM
TRICUSPIDARIA LANCEOLATA
*Evergreen shrub*

A slightly tender shrub with dense growth and an upright stance. The leaves are narrow, long, deep green, and leathery. The pendent, lantern-like, waxy, crimson flowers are borne on stems that are up to 3in (7.5cm) long from mid-spring to early summer.

- ❊ HEIGHT 10–15ft (3–4.5m)
- ❊ SPREAD 6–10ft (1.8–3m)
- ❊ SITUATION Partial shade, preferably in the shelter of a warm wall
- ❊ SOIL Fertile, moisture-retentive, and lime-free
- ❊ HARDINESS 10° to 0°F (-12° to -17°C)
- ❊ ZONES 6–8

## RHODODENDRON 'ELIZABETH'
HYBRID RHODODENDRON
*Evergreen shrub*

A superb, early-flowering small shrub with trusses bearing six to nine trumpet-shaped, rich scarlet flowers, each up to 3in (7.5cm) long, during spring.

There are several other evergreen hybrids, in colors including lavender-blue, primrose-yellow, white, and pink.

- ❋ HEIGHT 2–3ft (60–90cm)
- ❋ SPREAD 3–6ft (90cm–1.8m)
- ❋ SITUATION Light shade and shelter from cold wind
- ❋ SOIL Light, well-drained, but moisture-retentive, and slightly acid
- ❋ HARDINESS 20° to 10°F (-6° to -12°C)
- ❋ ZONES 5–7

## RIBES SANGUINEUM 'PULBOROUGH SCARLET'
WINTER CURRANT
*Deciduous shrub*

A dense shrub with mid- to deep green leaves and pendulous clusters, up to 4in (10cm) long, of deep rose-red flowers during spring. The flowers are a rich cardinal-red when in bud.

Other varieties have crimson flowers, while 'Brocklebankii' has golden-yellow foliage and pale pink flowers.

- ❋ HEIGHT 6–7ft (1.8–2.1m)
- ❋ SPREAD 5–6ft (1.5–1.8m)
- ❋ SITUATION Full sun or light shade
- ❋ SOIL Well-drained
- ❋ HARDINESS 0° to -10°F (-17° to -23°C)
- ❋ ZONES 5–7

**CLEMATIS**
**'VILLE DE LYON'**
LARGE-FLOWERED CLEMATIS
*Deciduous climber*

This glorious large-flowered climber is just one of a large group of clematis that drench trellises in color. This variety bears large, bright carmine-red flowers from midsummer to fall. The color of each flower is deeper at its edges, while the centers are packed with golden stamens.

☀ HEIGHT 5–7ft (1.5–2.1m)

☀ SPREAD 4–5ft (1.2–1.5m)

☀ SITUATION Full sun and an open position; ensure that the roots are shaded from strong sunlight

☀ SOIL Slightly chalky, and well-drained but moisture-retentive

☀ HARDINESS 0° to -10°F (-17° to -23°C)

☀ ZONES 3–8

**LONICERA × BROWNII**
**'DROPMORE SCARLET'**
BROWN'S HONEYSUCKLE
*Semievergreen climber*

A strong-growing climber with mid-green leaves that have a blue tinge on their upper surfaces. From midsummer to fall it bears terminal clusters of bright scarlet, tubular flowers.

No regular pruning is needed.

☀ HEIGHT 10–15ft (3–4.5m)

☀ SPREAD 6–12ft (1.8–3.6m)

☀ SITUATION Light shade, with the roots shaded from strong sunlight

☀ SOIL Fertile, and well-drained but moisture-retentive

☀ HARDINESS -10° to -20°F (-23° to -28°C)

☀ ZONES 6–8

*LONICERA × BROWNII 'DROPMORE SCARLET'*

## ROSA
### 'JOSEPHINE BRUCE, CLIMBING'
CLIMBING ROSE
*Deciduous climber*

This attractive climber is a sport
from the well-known Hybrid Tea
rose 'Josephine Bruce', which is
widely grown in rose borders. It is a
climber with stiff, branching
growth and double, fragrant, pure
crimson flowers during early
summer. Sometimes flowering is
repeated later in the season.

- ❋ HEIGHT 15ft (4.5m)
- ❋ SPREAD 10ft (3m)
- ❋ SITUATION Full sun and an
  open position
- ❋ SOIL Well-drained
- ❋ HARDINESS 10° to 0°F
  (-12° to -17°C)
- ❋ ZONES 5–9

## TROPAEOLUM SPECIOSUM
VERMILION NASTURTIUM
*Deciduous climber*

A spectacular perennial climber
with a creeping, rhizomatous
rootstock; in fall the entire plant
dies down to soil level.

The plant has a sprawling nature,
with downy and hairy stems
bearing six-lobed, mid-green
leaves. From midsummer to early
fall it bears long-stemmed,
trumpetlike, scarlet flowers.

- ❋ HEIGHT 10–15ft (3–4.5m)
- ❋ SPREAD 2½–3¼ft (75cm–1m)
- ❋ SITUATION Full sun, but the roots
  require shade from strong sunlight
- ❋ SOIL Fertile, and neutral or slightly
  acid, moisture-retentive but
  well-drained
- ❋ HARDINESS 20° to 10°F
  (-6° to -12°C)
- ❋ ZONES 7–10

### COTONEASTER MICROPHYLLUS
*Evergreen shrub*

A distinctive, low-growing shrub with wide-spreading branches bearing small, dark green, glossy leaves. During late spring and early summer it produces small, white flowers, either singly or in twos or threes. These are followed by round, scarlet berries.

This makes an ideal shrub for covering banks.

- ❄ HEIGHT 6in (15cm)
- ❄ SPREAD 5–7ft (1.5–2.1m)
- ❄ SITUATION Full sun
- ❄ SOIL Well-drained
- ❄ HARDINESS -10° to -20°F (-23° to -28°C)
- ❄ ZONES 5–8

### ROSA MOYESII
MOYES ROSE
*Deciduous shrub*

A vigorous, bushlike rose with red, slightly prickly stems and dark green leaves. During early summer it bears pink to blood-red, single flowers, each about 2in (5cm) across. The well-known flagon-shaped, glossy red fruits appear in lax clusters during fall. They are usually known as heps or hips.

- ❄ HEIGHT 6–9ft (1.8–2.7m)
- ❄ SPREAD 6–9ft (1.8–2.7m)
- ❄ SITUATION Full sun and an open position
- ❄ SOIL Well-drained
- ❄ HARDINESS -10° to -20°F (-23° to -28°C)
- ❄ ZONES 5–8

## SKIMMIA JAPONICA
*Evergreen shrub*

A rounded shrub with leathery, pale-green leaves and fragrant, creamy white, small, and starlike flowers in terminal clusters up to 3in (7.5cm) long during spring.

The bright red fruits are at their very best in late summer and in early fall.

❋ HEIGHT 3–5ft (90cm–1.5m)

❋ SPREAD 5–6ft (1.5–1.8m)

❋ SITUATION Full sun or partial shade; it grows best in lime-free soil

❋ SOIL Well-drained

❋ HARDINESS 10° to 0°F (-12° to -17°C)

❋ ZONES 7–8

## VIBURNUM OPULUS
EUROPEAN CRANBERRY-BUSH
*Deciduous shrub*

A large, bushy, and upright shrub with gray stems bearing dark green, maplelike leaves and white, heavily scented flowers in 2–3in (5–7.5cm) wide, flat heads during early summer; sometimes they appear in midsummer. These are followed by translucent red berries in fall.

No regular pruning is needed, but thin out congested shrubs immediately the flowers fade.

❋ HEIGHT 10–15ft (3–4.5m)

❋ SPREAD 12–15ft (3.6–4.5m)

❋ SITUATION Full sun and shelter from strong, cold winds

❋ SOIL Fertile, and moisture-retentive but well-drained

❋ HARDINESS -30° to -40°F (-34° to -40°C )

❋ ZONES 3–8

*Bright red flowers look good all year round.*

# index for red

*See the following pages for other plants with several varieties, including red:*

# PINK

*Many winter-flowering shrubs are
pale pink—and when viewed against
a pale blue sky, they positively glow.*

## the color pink
# pink plants

Pink is not a true color or hue within the spectrum but is actually a tint of red; however, it appears in the garden in so many different guises that it really needs to be considered separately. Decide which particular shades of pink you like most: the light pinks, lavenders, and gray; shocking pink and deep purple; or a scattering of pale buff, pink, peach, and apricot.

*The silvery pink flowers of this geranium form one example of the lighter pinks that are available for the garden.*

There are thousands of pink flowers to be found, ranging from the pale pink of *Campanula lactiflora* 'Loddon Anna' through the light pink of *Persicaria bistorta* 'Superbum' and many of the pink sweet peas to the rich pink of *Hyacinthus* 'Pink Pearl' and *Cosmos* 'Sonata'. Add a touch of orange and you have a peachy and salmon pink, as displayed in *Geranium* × *oxonianum* 'Wargrave Pink'. Alternatively, a touch of blue gives us *Phlox paniculata* 'Eve Cullum' and the shocking pink of *Cistus* × *pulverulentus* 'Sunset'.

Unbelievably, there are even some plants with pink leaves, or at least pink-, white- and-green variegated leaves; these include the climbers *Actinidia kolomikta* and *Ampelopsis brevipedunculata* 'Elegans', as well as the shrub *Spiraea japonica* 'Anthony Watererer'. There are several plants that produce pink fruits even if, like the pink-and-white foliage plants, there was insufficient space to give them a place in the plant directory. These include *Gaultheria mucronata* and *Sorbus vilmorinii*.

*LUPINUS 'THE CHATELAINE'*

## COLOR HARMONIES

As with the full color of red, pink should harmonize with orange and mauve and act as an opposite color to green. But somehow this does not always work, and it needs to be a peachy pink with orange and a bluey pink with mauve. The opposites of pink and green are not nearly as dramatic as red and green, but a bed of pink roses is extremely easy on the eye. Pink and lavender with gray foliage is another restful combination, and this forms the classic grouping of colors mentioned previously that seems to shine out of a dull, wet summer's day, but which fades to a gray shadow in bright sunlight.

## USING PINK IN YOUR GARDEN

Late spring is a prime season for pink flowers: the large range of pink tulips coming at the same time as clouds of pink cherry blossom, following on from the early start of yellow daffodils, purple crocuses, and blue scillas. Mix pink with true blue in the spring for a very pretty effect—pink hyacinths and tulips with forget-me-nots and blue pansies. In summer borders pink peonies and roses with blue and purple delphiniums make another classic combination, particularly when, in later summer, the same border is planted with pink phlox and Japanese anemones and with lavender New York daisies.

*Different shades of pink, such as those of* Allium unifolium *and* Gladiolus communis byzantinus, *harmonize well when planted with purple flowers.*

**'POMPONETTE ROSE'**
ENGLISH DAISY
*Biennial*

A superb form of the common daisy, with large, rose-colored flowers packed with small, quilled petals, mainly in spring and early summer, but often continuously throughout the summer.

Other colors in this quilled form include red and white.

- ❋ HEIGHT 4–6in (10–15cm)
- ❋ SPREAD 5–6in (13–15cm)
- ❋ SITUATION Full sun or partial shade
- ❋ SOIL Fertile, and moisture-retentive but well-drained
- ❋ HARDINESS Tolerates temperatures down to about 20°F (-6°C)
- ❋ ZONES 4–9

COSMOS
**'SONATA PINK SHADES'**
COSMOS
*Semihardy annual*

This attractive annual, with finely cut, mid-green leaves, develops masses of 3in (7.5cm) wide, pink flowers on strong stems during late summer and into early fall.

This variety is short and well suited for more exposed positions.

- ❋ HEIGHT 2ft (60cm)
- ❋ SPREAD 1¼–1½ft (38–45cm)
- ❋ SITUATION Full sun
- ❋ SOIL Light and well-drained
- ❋ HARDINESS Will not tolerate temperatures below 32°F (0°C)
- ❋ ZONES Semihardy, warm-season annual in zones 3–10

COSMOS 'SONATA PINK SHADES'

**'SILVER CUP'**
**LAVATERA ROSEA 'SILVER CUP'**
HERB TREE-MALLOW
*Hardy annual*

This widely grown hardy annual creates a feast of 4in (10cm) wide, glowing pink flowers from midsummer to early fall. It is a variety that survives both cold and wet seasons.

- ☀ **HEIGHT** 1¾–2ft (50–60cm)
- ☀ **SPREAD** 1½–1¾ft (45–50cm)
- ☀ **SITUATION** Full sun and slight shelter
- ☀ **SOIL** Light and well-drained; excessively rich and moist soil encourages lush leaf growth
- ☀ **HARDINESS** Tolerates slight frost
- ☀ **ZONES** Hardy, cool-season annual in zones 2–11

PETUNIA
**'RESISTO PINK'**
PETUNIA
*Semihardy annual*

Derived from *Petunia × hybrida*, this semihardy perennial is invariably grown as a semihardy annual for blanketing borders and containers with color from early summer to the frosts of fall. This variety is derived from the multiflora group and has large, 2in (5cm) wide, showy, and funnel-shaped pink flowers.

- ☀ **HEIGHT** 8–12in (20–30cm)
- ☀ **SPREAD** 10–12in (25–30cm)
- ☀ **SITUATION** Full sun
- ☀ **SOIL** Light and well-drained; excessively rich soil combined with too much soil-moisture encourages lush growth at the expense of flowers
- ☀ **HARDINESS** Will not tolerate temperatures below 32°F (0°C)
- ☀ **ZONES** Tender perennial, grown as a summer annual in zones 2–8; as a winter annual in deserts of zones 9–11

COLCHICUM
**'WATER LILY'**
FALL-CROCUS
*Corm*

An easily grown cormous plant
with mauve-pink double flowers
during early and mid-fall.
Sometimes this superb hybrid is
sold as a form of *Colchicum
speciosum*. There are several forms of
both *C. speciosum* and *C. fallale*,
another fall-flowering species, with
flowers in shades of pink, mauve,
lilac-rose, violet-purple, and white.

Plant the corms 3–4in
(7.5–10cm) deep in clusters of
five or six.

☀ HEIGHT 6in (15cm)

☀ SPREAD Plant corms 9in (23cm) apart

☀ SITUATION Full sun or dappled light

☀ SOIL Well-drained but moisture-
retentive

☀ HARDINESS -10° to -20°F
(-23° to -28°C)

☀ ZONES 5–9

ERYTHRONIUM DENS-CANIS
**'ROSE QUEEN'**
DOGTOOTH FAWN-LILY
*Bulb*

An informal and somewhat
sprawling bulbous plant with
bluish-green leaves blotched brown
or gray. During mid- and late
spring it develops 2–3in (5–7.5cm)
wide, pink flowers.

It is a variable species, with
flowers from white through rose to
deep cyclamen.

☀ HEIGHT 6in (15cm)

☀ SPREAD Plant bulbs 4–6in
(10–15cm) apart

☀ SITUATION Dappled light

☀ SOIL Fertile, and moisture-retentive
but well-drained

☀ HARDINESS -30° to -40°F
(-34° to -40°C)

☀ ZONES 3–8

A distinctive bulbous plant, with soldierlike, upright spires that are packed with pink flowers during late spring.

Plant the bulbs 5–6in (13–15cm) deep in early fall for flowering in spring. After flowering the bulbs should be dug up, so that summer-flowering plants can be put in their place.

Other varieties extend the color range to white, yellow, orange, red, and blue.

* HEIGHT 6–9in (15–23cm)
* SPREAD Plant bulbs 6–8in (15–20cm) apart
* SITUATION Full sun
* SOIL Moderately fertile, and moisture-retentive but well-drained
* HARDINESS 20° to 10°F (-6° to -12°C)
* ZONES 3–7

This attractive bulbous plant has gray-green, lance-shaped leaves and large, rosy pink flowers with blunt-pointed petals. It is a variable species, usually containing red or scarlet flowers.

Plant the bulbs in fall, setting them 5–6in (13–15cm) deep in most soils, but slightly deeper in light, sandy types.

* HEIGHT 12–18in (30–45cm)
* SPREAD Plant bulbs 6in (15cm) apart
* SITUATION Full sun and shelter from strong, cold wind
* SOIL Well-drained but moisture-retentive
* HARDINESS -10° to -20°F (-23° to -28°C)
* ZONES 4–8

## CAMPANULA LACTIFLORA
### 'LODDON ANNA'
MILKY BELLFLOWER
*Herbaceous perennial*

This perennial forms a clump of upright stems packed with light green leaves and branching heads of bell-shaped, soft mushroom-pink flowers during early and midsummer, and sometimes later.

There are several related varieties, which come in shades of blue, pink, and lavender.

- ❋ HEIGHT 3¼–4ft (1–1.2m)
- ❋ SPREAD 1¼–1½ft (38–45cm)
- ❋ SITUATION Full sun or partial shade
- ❋ SOIL Fertile and well-drained
- ❋ HARDINESS -10° to -20°F (-23° to -28°C)
- ❋ ZONES 5–7

## GERANIUM × OXONIANUM
### 'WARGRAVE PINK'
**GERANIUM ENDRESSII**
**'WARGRAVE PINK'**
ENDRES CRANESBILL
*Herbaceous perennial*

A clump-forming border geranium with deeply lobed, mid-green leaves and silvery pink, saucer-shaped flowers, each about 1in (2.5cm) across, from early to late summer. There are several other superb pink varieties.

This plant is ideal for planting to smother the soil with foliage.

- ❋ HEIGHT 1½ft (45cm)
- ❋ SPREAD 1¼–1½ft (38–45cm)
- ❋ SITUATION Full sun or partial shade
- ❋ SOIL Well-drained but moisture-retentive
- ❋ HARDINESS -10° to -20°F (-23° to -28°C)
- ❋ ZONES 3–8

**LUPINUS**
**'THE CHATELAINE'**
LUPINE
*Herbaceous perennial*

A magnificent border plant with leaves formed of many mid-green leaflets. Upright stems, about 2ft (60cm) tall, develop spires packed with bicolored, white-and-pink flowers during early and midsummer.

There are many varieties, in a wide color range, including mixtures of white, blue, pink, violet, red, and yellow.

☀ HEIGHT 3–3¾ft (90cm–1m)

☀ SPREAD 2–2½ft (60–75cm)

☀ SITUATION Full sun or partial shade

☀ SOIL Light, neutral, or slightly acid

☀ HARDINESS -10° to -20°F
  (-23° to -28°C)

☀ ZONES 4–9

**LYCHNIS FLOS-JOVIS**
**AGROSTEMMA FLOS-JOVIS**
FLOWER-OF-LOVE
*Herbaceous perennial*

A pretty, somewhat lax border plant with branched stems bearing thick, lancelike, silver or gray leaves. From early to late summer it creates a mass of bright pink, salver-shaped flowers.

☀ HEIGHT 1¾–2ft (50–60cm)

☀ SPREAD 9–12in (23–30cm)

☀ SITUATION Full sun or light shade

☀ SOIL Well-drained

☀ HARDINESS 0° to -10°F
  (-17° to -23°C)

☀ ZONES 4–8

LUPINUS 'THE CHATELAINE'

**herbaceous perennials** 121

## LYTHRUM VIRGATUM
### 'THE ROCKET'
LOOSESTRIFE
*Herbaceous perennial*

A slender and elegant border
plant with wiry stems that are well
clothed with narrow, pointed, mid-
green leaves. From early summer
to early fall it bears deep
rose-pink, star-shaped flowers
in spirelike heads.

There are other pink varieties.

☀ HEIGHT 2–3ft (60–90cm)

☀ SPREAD 1¼–1½ft (38–45cm)

☀ SITUATION Full sun or light shade

☀ SOIL Well-drained but
moisture-retentive

☀ HARDINESS -10° to -20°F
(-23° to -28°C)

☀ ZONES 3–9

## PAEONIA LACTIFLORA
### 'SARAH BERNHARDT'
PAEONIA ALBIFLORA
'SARAH BERNHARDT'
CHINESE PEONY
*Herbaceous perennial*

A spectacular border plant with
large, mid- to deep green leaves
and magnificent double, slightly
scented, apple-blossom pink
flowers. Each of these is about
6in (15cm) wide, from late
spring to midsummer.

There are many varieties,
extending the color range to rose–
purple, crimson, red, and white.

☀ HEIGHT 3ft (90cm)

☀ SPREAD 3ft (90cm)

☀ SITUATION Full sun or partial shade

☀ SOIL Moisture-retentive but well-
drained and fertile

☀ HARDINESS 10° to 0°F
(-12° to -17°C)

☀ ZONES 2–8

PERSICARIA BISTORTA
**'SUPERBUM'**
POLYGONUM BISTORTA 'SUPERBUM'
SNAKEWEED
*Herbaceous perennial*

A ground-covering and spreading
border plant with light green leaves
surmounted, between late spring
and midsummer, with 6in (15cm)
high spires tightly packed with
rose-pink flowers.

* HEIGHT 2½–3ft (75–90cm)
* SPREAD 2–2½ft (60–75cm)
* SITUATION Full sun or partial shade
* SOIL Fertile and moisture-retentive
* HARDINESS -20° to -30°F
    (-28° to -34°C)
* ZONES 3–8

PHLOX PANICULATA
**'EVA CULLUM'**
PHLOX DECUSSATA 'EVA CULLUM'
GARDEN PHLOX
*Herbaceous perennial*

A clump-forming border plant
with upright stems bearing lance-
shaped, mid-green leaves. From
midsummer to early fall pink
flowers about 1in (2.5cm) across
are borne in dense heads up to
6in (15cm) long.

There are many varieties,
extending the color range to white,
violet-purple, claret-red, and
salmon-orange.

* HEIGHT 3ft (90cm)
* SPREAD 1½–1¾ft (45–50cm)
* SITUATION Full sun or partial shade
* SOIL Fertile, and moisture-retentive
    but well-drained
* HARDINESS -20° to -30°F
    (-28° to -34°C)
* ZONES 4–8

PHYSOSTEGIA VIRGINIANA
'VIVID'
DRACOCEPHALUM VIRGINIANUM
'VIVID'
VIRGINIA LION'S-HEART
*Herbaceous perennial*

A distinctive border plant with upright stems packed with sharply toothed, mid-green, lance-shaped leaves. During mid- and late summer it produces 5in (13cm) long spikes of deep pink flowers. When pushed to one side, these flowers remain in position.

There are several other varieties, extending the color range to white and deep lilac-purple.

☀ HEIGHT 2½–4ft (75cm–1.2m)
☀ SPREAD 2ft (60cm)
☀ SITUATION Full sun or partial shade
☀ SOIL Well-drained but moisture-retentive
☀ HARDINESS -20° to -30°F (-28° to -34°C)
☀ ZONES 2–9

SCHIZOSTYLIS COCCINEA
'VISCOUNTESS BYNG'
CRIMSON-FLAG
*Herbaceous perennial*

This rhizomatous-rooted perennial is a distinctive border plant. It creates a wealth of green, sword-like, and flat leaves that, during mid-fall, are surmounted by 9in (23cm) long spikes of pale pink, star-shaped flowers, each 1⅜in (36mm) wide.

There are other varieties, in colors including pearly white and deep red.

☀ HEIGHT 3ft (90cm)
☀ SPREAD 9–12in (23–30cm)
☀ SITUATION Full sun and shelter from cold wind
☀ SOIL Fertile and moisture-retentive
☀ HARDINESS 0° to -10°F (-17° to -23°C)
☀ ZONES 7–10

**SEDUM SPECTABILE**
**'BRILLIANT'**
SHOWY SEDUM
*Border perennial*

A distinctive plant with large,
thick, white-green, stem-clasping,
succulent leaves and deep rose,
star-shaped flowers borne in dense,
nearly flat heads up to 5in (13cm)
wide, from late summer until
mid-fall.

Other varieties have deep
carmine-red, carmine, or
pink flowers.

✳ HEIGHT 1–1½ft (30–45cm)

✳ SPREAD 1½ft (45cm)

✳ SITUATION Full sun

✳ SOIL Light and well-drained

✳ HARDINESS 10° to 0°F
  (-12° to -17°C)

✳ ZONES 3–10

**SIDALCEA**
**'PARTY GIRL'**
CHECKER-MALLOW
*Herbaceous perennial*

A spectacular border plant with
shallowly lobed, kidney-shaped,
mid-green lower leaves. From early
to late summer the plant bears tall
stems with long spires packed with
2in (5cm) wide, pink flowers.

✳ HEIGHT 2½–3ft (75–90cm)

✳ SPREAD 1½ft (45cm)

✳ SITUATION Full sun

✳ SOIL Well-drained but
  moisture-retentive

✳ HARDINESS 0° to -10°F
  (-17° to -23°C)

✳ ZONES 5–7

## CISTUS 'SUNSET'
CISTUS × PULVERULENTUS
'SUNSET'
ROCK-ROSE
*Evergreen shrub*

A dense, compact, low-growing shrub with small, undulating, sage-green leaves and 1½–2in (36–50mm) wide, rose-pink flowers in early and midsummer, but also at intervals until fall.

No regular pruning is needed, other than cutting out frost-damaged shoots in late winter or early spring.

☀ HEIGHT 2–2½ft (60–75cm)

☀ SPREAD 2–3ft (60–90cm)

☀ SITUATION Full sun and shelter from cold wind

☀ SOIL Well-drained; it grows well in poor soil

☀ HARDINESS 20° to 10°F (-6° to -12°C)

☀ ZONES 8–10

## DEUTZIA × ELEGANTISSIMIMA 'ROSEALIND'
*Deciduous shrub*

An upright and bushy shrub with lance-shaped, pointed, matt green leaves and fragrant, starlike, deep carmine-pink flowers in clusters on arching branches during late spring and early summer.

Prune in midsummer; cut out old flowering stems to ground level to encourage the development of new shoots.

☀ HEIGHT 4–5ft (1.2–1.5m)

☀ SPREAD 4–5ft (1.2–1.5m)

☀ SITUATION Full sun or dappled light

☀ SOIL Well-drained

☀ HARDINESS 0° to -10°F (-17° to -23°C)

☀ ZONES 4–8

## HIBISCUS SYRIACUS 'WOODBRIDGE'
SHRUB ALTHEA
*Deciduous shrub*

Bushy and upright, with rich green, three-lobed, and coarsely toothed leaves. From midsummer to early fall it bears 3in (7.5cm) wide, rose-pink flowers.

Other varieties extend the color range to violet-blue, white with red centers, wine-red, and rose-pink.

No regular pruning is needed, other than shortening long shoots immediately the shrub finishes flowering. Additionally, cut out frost-damaged shoot-tips in spring.

❋ HEIGHT 6–10ft (1.8–3m)
❋ SPREAD 4–6ft (1.2–1.8m)
❋ SITUATION Full sun or light shade, and shelter from cold wind
❋ SOIL Fertile, and well-drained but moisture-retentive
❋ HARDINESS -10° to -20°F (-23° to -28°C)
❋ ZONES 5–8

## KALMIA LATIFOLIA
MOUNTAIN-LAUREL
*Evergreen shrub*

A bushy shrub with leathery and glossy, lance-shaped, mid-green leaves and saucer-shaped, bright pink flowers borne in clusters about 4in (10cm) across during early summer. The variety 'Clementine Churchill' has rich, rosy-red flowers.

No regular pruning is needed, other than removing any old flower heads.

❋ HEIGHT 6–10ft (1.8–3m)
❋ SPREAD 6–8ft (1.8–2.4m)
❋ SITUATION Partial shade
❋ SOIL Moisture-retentive, lime-free, cool, and peaty
❋ HARDINESS -20° to -30°F (-28° to -34°C)
❋ ZONES 4–9

**KOLKWITZIA AMABILIS
'PINK CLOUD'**
BEAUTYBUSH
*Deciduous shrub*

An upright, arching, and slightly
twiggy shrub with broadly oval,
dark green leaves and peeling
brown bark. During early summer
it bears masses of foxglovelike,
pink flowers.

After the flowers fade, use pruners
to remove some of the older stems.

☀ HEIGHT 6–10ft (1.8–3m)
☀ SPREAD 5–8ft (1.5–2.4m)
☀ SITUATION Full sun or light shade
☀ SOIL Well-drained but
   moisture-retentive
☀ HARDINESS -20° to -30°F
   (-28° to -34°C)
☀ ZONES 4–8

**MAGNOLIA × SOULANGEANA
'RUSTICA RUBRA'**
**MAGNOLIA × SOULANGEANA
'RUBRA'**
SAUCER MAGNOLIA
*Deciduous tree*

An impressive, slow-growing tree,
with a spreading nature and large,
mid-green, broad, lance-shaped
leaves with downy undersides.
During mid- and late spring it
bears chalice-shaped, rosy red
flowers, which open before the
leaves unfurl.

No regular pruning is needed.

☀ HEIGHT 10–15ft (3–4.5m)
☀ SPREAD 10–18ft (3–5.4m)
☀ SITUATION Full sun or light shade,
   and shelter from strong, cold wind
☀ SOIL Deeply prepared, and well-
   drained but moisture-retentive
☀ HARDINESS -10° to -20°F
   (-23° to -28°C)
☀ ZONES 4–9

**PRUNUS TENELLA**
**'FIRE HILL'**
RUSSIAN ALMOND
*Deciduous shrub*

A low and bushy deciduous shrub with shiny, dark green leaves and erect stems bearing masses of brilliant rose-red flowers during mid- and late spring.

No regular pruning is needed.

☀ HEIGHT 3–5ft (90cm–1.5m)

☀ SPREAD 4–5ft (1.2–1.5m)

☀ SITUATION Full sun and shelter from strong, cold wind

☀ SOIL Well-drained but moisture-retentive, and neutral or slightly chalky

☀ HARDINESS -40° to -50°F (-40° to -45°C)

☀ ZONES 2–6

**ROSA**
**'FELICIA'**
HYBRID MUSK ROSE
*Deciduous shrub*

This cluster-flowered, hybrid musk rose has the appearance and nature of a Hybrid Tea rose. During late summer and until the first frosts of fall it bears clusters of fragrant, silvery salmon-pink, semidouble flowers.

There are many other hybrid musk roses, extending the color range to mauve-crimson, crimson-scarlet, soft yellow, and pure white.

☀ HEIGHT 5ft (1.5m)

☀ SPREAD 5–7ft (1.5–2.1m)

☀ SITUATION Full sun and an open position, away from overhanging trees

☀ SOIL Well-drained but moisture-retentive

☀ HARDINESS 10° to 0°F (-12° to -17°C)

☀ ZONES 6–9

**CLEMATIS MONTANA**
**'ELIZABETH'**
ANEMONE CLEMATIS
*Deciduous climber*

A vigorous climber with dark green leaves formed of three leaflets and masses of 2–2½in (5–6.5cm) wide, fragrant, light pink flowers during late spring and early summer.

There are several varieties in a color range including white and lilac-rose.

No regular pruning is needed, other than occasionally trimming back excessively large plants.

☀ HEIGHT 18–25ft (5.4–7.5m)

☀ SPREAD 15–20ft (4.5–6m)

☀ SITUATION Sunny, but with shade for the roots; plant low-growing plants around its base

☀ SOIL Fertile, neutral, or slightly alkaline, well-drained but moisture-retentive

☀ HARDINESS 0° to -10°F (-17° to -23°C)

☀ ZONES 5–7

**LAPAGERIA ROSEA**
RED CHILE-BELLS
*Evergreen climbing shrub*

A warmth-loving wall shrub with an erect habit and leathery, dark green leaves. From midsummer to fall it becomes drenched with pendent, bell-shaped, rose-crimson flowers up to 3in (7.5cm) long. In cold areas this shrub is best grown in a large greenhouse.

No regular pruning is needed, other than to thin out weak shoots in spring.

☀ HEIGHT 10–15ft (3–4.5m)

☀ SPREAD 6–8ft (1.8–2.4m)

☀ SITUATION Full sun or partial light shade, and a position against a sunny, wind-sheltered wall; it does best where there is slight shade during the hottest part of the day

☀ SOIL Neutral or slightly acid, and moisture-retentive but well-drained

☀ HARDINESS 30° to 20°F (-1° to -6°C)

☀ ZONES 9–11

## LATHYRUS ODORATUS
### 'ANNIVERSARY'
SWEET PEA
*Hardy annual*

An annual climber with fragrant, 1in (2.5cm) wide, soft white flowers with rose-pink picotee edges.

There are many varieties of this sweet pea, including shades of red, pink, blue, purple, and white.

❊ HEIGHT 6–10ft (1.8–3m)
❊ SPREAD 2–4ft (60cm–1.2m)
❊ SITUATION Full sun
❊ SOIL Fertile, and moisture-retentive but well-drained; slightly alkaline
❊ HARDINESS Tolerates slight frost
❊ ZONES Hardy, cool-season annual in zones 2–11

## ROSA
### 'NEW DAWN'
CLIMBING ROSE
*Deciduous climber*

This bushy and moderately vigorous Modern Climber creates a mass of glossy leaves and large sprays of medium-size, silvery blush-pink flowers, which reveal a fruity fragrance.

It is a forerunner of modern perpetual-flowering climbers, and its flowers are produced almost continuously throughout the summer.

❊ HEIGHT 9ft (2.7m)
❊ SPREAD 7–8ft (2.1–2.4m)
❊ SITUATION Full sun or partial shade, with good circulation of the air
❊ SOIL Well-drained but moisture-retentive
❊ HARDINESS 10° to 0°F (-12° to -17°C)
❊ ZONES 5–9

ROSA 'NEW DAWN'

# index for pink

*See the following pages for other plants with several varieties, including pink:*

# PURPLE

*Purple ranges in tone from soft
lilac to the rich and
exotic emperor-purples.*

# the color purple
# purple plants

*The violet-purple of Aubrieta 'Doctor Mules' is just one of the shades of purple available from this pretty plant.*

The name purple is given to a range of differently perceived colors, varying from the pinky purples and mauves of the flowers of *Aubrieta deltoidea*, which drapes our walls so prettily in the spring, through the true emperor-purples found in the flowers of *Campanula glomerata* and *Salvia × sylvestris* 'May Night' to the soft lilacs of sage, rosemary, and many of the lavenders. It can be difficult to decide whether a flower is blue or lilac, and books are not always clear on this point. In this book you will find all but the true blues in the purple section.

In foliage, purple can be perceived as plum-colored where there is a strong deep red element, as in *Cotinus coggygria* 'Royal Purple' and *Heuchera micrantha* 'Palace Purple', but is nearer true purple in the leaves of *Vitis vinifera* 'Purpurea'. There are also a few purple fruits—too few to include as a section in the plant directory—and ripe black grapes and damsons are in fact deep purple in color; other black fruits, such as those of *Prunus laurocerasus*, have a purple blush.

## COLOR HARMONIES

Most of the tints, tones, and shades of purple can be planted together as long as the reddest of the bright mauves are not used. The adjacent colors to purple are

blue and red, and both harmonies work well in flower and foliage color. Blue and purple flowers are attractive together, but being "cool" colors they appear to retreat into the surrounding greens, so may not make enough impact. The combination of purple and red (as in fuchsias) is seen in many of the plants found in Mediterranean countries. The secret to this color harmony is to make sure that you use a true red and not a scarlet or orange-red. The opposite and complementary color to purple is yellow and, as explained *(see p.39)*, there are lots of planting associations.

## USING PURPLE IN YOUR GARDEN

Try a different approach by concentrating on a majority of purple flowers offset by just a few creamy yellow or primrose flowers. Or use the tints of each of the colors plus some gray foliage—it is easy to create an attractive herb garden combining yellow and purple sage, golden marjoram with its soft purple flowers, cotton lavenders, rosemary, and thyme.

*The blue leaves of these cabbages make a "cool" harmony with the surrounding purple flowers.*

LAVANDULA ANGUSTIFOLIA

135

## CALLISTEPHUS CHINENSIS
### 'MILADY BLUE'
CHINA ASTER
*Semihardy annual*

A well-known, erect but bushy
semihardy annual with coarsely
toothed, mid-green leaves and
masses of large, daisylike, deep
purple-blue flowers containing a
hint of violet, from midsummer to
the frosts of fall.

There are many varieties, in a
range of colors including shades of
pink, red, purple, and white. These
also come in a range of heights.

- ☀ HEIGHT 10–12in (25–30cm)
- ☀ SPREAD 10–12in (25–30cm)
- ☀ SITUATION Full sun and shelter from
  strong, cold wind
- ☀ SOIL Moderately fertile and
  well-drained
- ☀ HARDINESS Will not tolerate
  temperatures below 32°F (0°C)
- ☀ ZONES Warm-season annual in
  zones 2–11

## HELIOTROPIUM ARBORESCENS
### 'MARINE'
HELIOTROPIUM PERUVIANUM
'MARINE'
COMMON HELIOTROPE
*Semihardy annual*

A familiar tender perennial, usually
grown as a semihardy annual. From
early summer to early fall this
compact variety develops fragrant,
forget-me-not-like, royal purple
flowers in heads about 3in
(7.5cm) wide.

There are several other varieties,
in colors ranging from dark violet
to lavender, and including white.

- ☀ HEIGHT 1½ft (45cm)
- ☀ SPREAD 1–1¼ft (30–38cm)
- ☀ SITUATION Full sun
- ☀ SOIL Fertile, and moisture-retentive
  but well-drained
- ☀ HARDINESS Will not tolerate
  temperatures below 32°F (0°C)
- ☀ ZONES Semihardy annual in zones
  2–9; protect in winter in zone 10;
  perennial in zone 11

## LIMONIUM SINUATUM
STATICE SINUATA
NOTCH-LEAF SEA-LAVENDER
*Semihardy annual*

This hardy perennial is usually grown as a semihardy annual to produce colorful and decorative heads from midsummer to early fall, which can be cut and dried to be used as "everlasting" flowers. The ordinary species develops clusters of blue and cream flowers, while this particular variety produces heads of purple flowers.

The range of varieties is wide and extends the color range to salmon, orange, yellow, pink, red, carmine, blue, and lavender.

※ HEIGHT 1½–1¾ft (45–50cm)

※ SPREAD 1ft (30cm)

※ SITUATION Full sun

※ SOIL Well-drained

※ HARDINESS Will not tolerate temperatures below 32°F (0°C)

※ ZONES Semihardy annual in zones 2–11

## PETUNIA
'PRIMETIME PLUM'
PETUNIA
*Semihardy annual*

Derived from *Petunia × hybrida*, this semihardy perennial is invariably grown as a semihardy annual for filling borders with color from early summer to the frosts of fall.

This superb variety has large, showy, funnel-shaped, plum-purple flowers. The range of varieties is wide and includes colors from white through to purple.

※ HEIGHT 8–12in (20–30cm)

※ SPREAD 10–12in (25–30cm)

※ SITUATION Full sun

※ SOIL Light and well-drained; excessively rich soil combined with too much soil moisture encourages lush growth at the expense of flowers

※ HARDINESS Will not tolerate temperatures below 32°F (0°C)

※ ZONES Tender perennial, grown as a summer annual in zones 2–8; as a winter annual in deserts of zones 9–11

## SALVIA FARINACEA 'VICTORIA'
MEALYCUP SAGE
*Semihardy annual*

This tender perennial is invariably grown as a semihardy annual. The leaves and stems are covered with a waxy dusting that creates a soft, gray-green appearance. From midsummer until fall it develops tall, narrow spires of vivid, purple-blue flowers.

There are several other varieties, with flowers in colors such as silvery white, deep lavender-blue, and soft clear-blue.

☀ **HEIGHT** 1½ft (45cm)

☀ **SPREAD** 1ft (30cm)

☀ **SITUATION** Full sun

☀ **SOIL** Fertile and well-drained

☀ **HARDINESS** Will not tolerate temperatures below 32°F (0°C)

☀ **ZONES** Tender perennial, grown as an annual in zones 2–7; as a perennial in zones 8–11

## VIOLA ULTIMA
HYBRID GARDEN PANSY
*Short-lived perennial*

A superb hybrid pansy, with a hardy-annual, biennial, or short-lived perennial nature, which is ideal for planting in containers as well as in borders. The rich violet-purple flowers are about 2in (5cm) wide and appear from fall through to spring.

This 'Ultimate' variety is part of a group of 25 separate and distinctive colors, most with clear hues and no blotches.

☀ **HEIGHT** 6–8in (15–20cm)

☀ **SPREAD** 10–12in (25–30cm)

☀ **SITUATION** Full sun or partial shade

☀ **SOIL** Fertile, and moisture-retentive but well-drained

☀ **HARDINESS** 20° to 10°F (-6° to -12°C)

☀ **ZONES** Hardy, cool-season annual in zones 2–11; as winter annual in zones 9–11

**ALLIUM AFLATUNENSE**
ALLIUM HOLLANDICUM
*Bulb*

A distinctive, bulbous plant that is ideal for planting in an herbaceous border. It develops glaucous, gray-green, straplike leaves and 3–4in (7.5–10cm) wide, starlike heads packed with violet flowers with dark central veins during late spring and early summer.

The variety 'Purple Sensation' reveals intense deep violet flowers.

☀ HEIGHT 2½ft (75cm)

☀ SPREAD Space bulbs 9in (23cm) apart

☀ SITUATION Full sun

☀ SOIL Well-drained

☀ HARDINESS 20° to 10°F
   (-6° to -12°C)

☀ ZONES 4–8

**CROCUS VERNUS**
**'PURPUREUS GRANDIFLORUS'**
CROCUS NEAPOLITANUS
'PURPUREUS GRANDIFLORUS'
COMMON CROCUS
*Corm*

The basic species is one of the parents of the many spring-flowering, large-flowered Dutch crocuses that are widely seen in our gardens. Once planted they create large clumps. This superb variety displays large, shining purple-blue flowers during early and mid-spring.

Other varieties extend the color range to white, silvery lilac, reddish-purple, and lavender-blue.

☀ HEIGHT 4–5in (10–13cm)

☀ SPREAD Space the corms 4in
   (10cm) apart

☀ SITUATION Full sun, or planted
   under deciduous trees

☀ SOIL Well-drained

☀ HARDINESS -20° to -30°F
   (-28° to -34°C )

☀ ZONES 3–8

## FRITILLARIA MELEAGRIS
GUINEA-HEN FLOWER
*Bulb*

A popular bulbous plant that is
ideal for growing in borders and
for naturalizing in short grass. It
has narrow, slightly glaucous, green
leaves. During mid- and late spring
it develops nodding, 1½in (36mm)
long, bell-shaped, white flowers,
which are almost completely
covered with distinctive purple-
checkered markings.

- ❊ HEIGHT 1–1½ft (30–45cm)
- ❊ SPREAD Space bulbs 4–6in
  (10–15cm) apart
- ❊ SITUATION Full sun
- ❊ SOIL Fertile, and moisture-retentive
  but well-drained
- ❊ HARDINESS -20° to -30°F
  (-28° to -34°C)
- ❊ ZONES 3–8

## IRIS RETICULATA
*Bulb*

A well-known bulbous iris with
a miniature stature. It is widely
grown in rock gardens, window
boxes, sink gardens, and pots on
patios. The four-ribbed, dark green,
somewhat grasslike leaves, with
lighter-colored tips, extend above
the late-winter and early-spring
flowers. These are up to 3in
(7.5cm) wide, deep blue-purple,
with orange blazes on some of
their petals.

- ❊ HEIGHT 6in (15cm)
- ❊ SPREAD Space bulbs 3–4in
  (7.5–10cm) apart
- ❊ SITUATION Full sun, with shelter
  from cold, blustery wind
- ❊ SOIL Light, well-drained, and
  slightly chalky
- ❊ HARDINESS 30° to 20°F
  (-1° to -6°C)
- ❊ ZONES 5–9

## ACANTHUS SPINOSUS
BEAR'S-BREECH
*Herbaceous perennial*

A distinctive, statuesque, and handsome plant with dark, shiny green, deeply cut, and spiny leaves. During mid- and late summer it develops tall spires of white and rosy purple flowers.

A related species, *Acanthus mollis*, has mauve-pink flowers, but the plant is slightly smaller.

* HEIGHT 3–3¼ft (90cm–1m)
* SPREAD 2–2½ft (60–75cm)
* SITUATION Full sun or light shade
* SOIL Deeply prepared, and well-drained but moisture-retentive
* HARDINESS 0° to -10°F (-17° to -23°C)
* ZONES 7–10

## ACONITUM NAPELLUS
ACONITE MONKSHOOD
*Herbaceous perennial*

With poisonous roots, this plant has dark green, deeply cut, and segmented leaves. During mid- and late summer it produces tall stems packed with helmet-shaped, deep purple-blue flowers.

There are several varieties, in colors including blue-and-white, deep violet-blue, and dark blue.

* HEIGHT 3¼ft (1m)
* SPREAD 1¼ft (38cm)
* SITUATION Partial shade
* SOIL Fertile, deeply prepared, and moisture-retentive
* HARDINESS 0° to -10°F (-17° to -23°C)
* ZONES 3–7

## ASTER × FRIKARTII 'MÖNCH'
*Herbaceous perennial*

This elegant aster, a hybrid between *Aster amellus* and *Aster thomsonii*, creates a mass of stout, branching stems that bear large, daisylike, deep lilac-blue flowers with orange centers from midsummer through to mid-fall.

There are many other herbaceous asters and some display spectacular daisylike flowers through to late fall or early winter.

- ❊ HEIGHT 3¼ft (1m)
- ❊ SPREAD 1¼–1½ft (38–45cm)
- ❊ SITUATION Full sun
- ❊ SOIL Fertile, and moisture-retentive but well-drained
- ❊ HARDINESS -20° to -30°F (-28° to -34°C)
- ❊ ZONES 5–8

## AUBRIETA 'DOCTOR MULES'
### AUBRIETA DELTOIDEA 'DR MULES'
PURPLE ROCK-CRESS
*Evergreen perennial*

This low-growing perennial develops a mass of small, hoary green leaves and cross-shaped, violet-purple flowers, each about 1½in (36mm) wide, from early spring to early summer.

Other varieties extend the color range to rosy lilac, with several shades of purple and blue. There is also a form with variegated leaves and purple flowers.

- ❊ HEIGHT 3–4in (7.5–10cm)
- ❊ SPREAD 1½–2ft (45–60cm)
- ❊ SITUATION Full sun
- ❊ SOIL Well-drained and, preferably, with a trace of lime
- ❊ HARDINESS 10° to 0°F (-12° to -17°C)
- ❊ ZONES 4–8

## CAMPANULA GLOMERATA 'SUPERBA'
CLUSTERED BELLFLOWER
*Herbaceous perennial*

This superb campanula has mid-green, tooth-edged leaves on erect stems. These contain dense heads packed with clusters of rich purple-violet flowers at their tops throughout summer and until the frosts of fall.

There is also a form of this perennial that has white flowers.

* HEIGHT 2½ft (75cm)
* SPREAD 1½–2ft (45–60cm)
* SITUATION Full sun or partial shade
* SOIL Fertile, and moisture-retentive but well-drained
* HARDINESS -40° to -50°F (-40° to -45°C)
* ZONES 3–8

## ECHINACEA PURPUREA
PURPLE ECHINACEA
*Herbaceous perennial*

A spectacular border plant with upright stems bearing rough-surfaced, slightly toothed, mid-green leaves and large, purple-crimson flowers, each up to 4in (10cm) wide, from midsummer through to the frosts of fall. Each flower has a distinctive conelike, orange center.

Other varieties extend the color range and include white with deep orange centers, and purple-rose and crimson-pink with mahogany-colored centers.

* HEIGHT 3–4ft (90cm–1.2m)
* SPREAD 1½–2ft (45–60cm)
* SITUATION Full sun
* SOIL Fertile and well-drained
* HARDINESS -30° to -40°F (-34° to -40°C)
* ZONES 3–8

CAMPANULA GLOMERATA

### ERIGERON
#### 'DARKEST OF ALL'
ERIGERON SPECIOSUS
'DARKEST OF ALL'
FLEABANE
*Herbaceous perennial*

A leafy, upright, but bushy plant with mid-green, spoon-shaped leaves and masses of large, daisylike, violet-blue flowers borne in terminal clusters from early to late summer.

There are several other superb varieties, which extend the color range to light mauve, blue, and deep pink.

* HEIGHT 1½–2ft (45–60cm)
* SPREAD 1–1¼ft (30–38cm)
* SITUATION Full sun
* SOIL Fertile, and moisture-retentive but well-drained
* HARDINESS -30° to -40°F (-34° to -40°C)
* ZONES 2–8

### GERANIUM HIMALAYENSE
#### 'PLENUM'
CRANESBILL
*Herbaceous perennial*

A bushy and carpet-forming perennial with mid-green leaves and masses of double, lavender-blue flowers in succession from early to late summer. Sometimes the flowers appear in late spring. The plant has a spreading rootstock.

There are many other herbaceous geraniums, with flowers in a wide range of colors, including pink through purple to blue.

* HEIGHT 10in (25cm)
* SPREAD 1½–2ft (45–60cm)
* SITUATION Sun or partial shade
* SOIL Well-drained
* HARDINESS -20° to -30°F (-28° to -34°C)
* ZONES 3–8

## LIRIOPE MUSCARI
LIRIOPE PLATYPHYLLA
BIG BLUE LILY-TURF
*Evergreen perennial*

An evergreen perennial, with a compact, clump-forming habit and stiff, broad, but grasslike, dark green leaves. From late summer to late fall it reveals clusters of lilac-mauve, bell-shaped flowers borne on long, wiry stems.

It is a resilient border plant and seldom fails to create a spectacular display there.

* HEIGHT 1–1½ft (30–45cm)
* SPREAD 15in (38cm)
* SITUATION Full sun or partial shade
* SOIL Fertile, light, well-drained, and slightly chalky; these plants are able to tolerate dry conditions
* HARDINESS 0° to -10°F (-17° to -23°C)
* ZONES 6–9

## ORIGANUM LAEVIGATUM
'HERRENHAUSEN'
ORNAMENTAL MARJORAM
*Herbaceous perennial*

A spreading and mat-forming border plant with oval, aromatic, dark green leaves and a profusion of violet, tubular flowers. These are surrounded by almost purple bracts from late summer to mid-fall. When young, the shoots are flushed purple.

The common species bears red-purple flowers.

* HEIGHT 1½–2ft (45–60cm)
* SPREAD 1½–2½ft (45–75cm)
* SITUATION Full sun
* SOIL Well-drained
* HARDINESS 20° to 10°F (-6° to -12°C)
* ZONES 5–9

## PENSTEMON
### 'RUSSIAN RIVER'
*Herbaceous perennial*

This slightly tender herbaceous perennial develops stem-clasping, lance-shaped, mid-green leaves. In warm areas it remains evergreen or semievergreen. Throughout summer and into early fall it reveals clusters of drooping, deep purple flowers.

There are several other varieties, with flowers in colors that include red, salmon-red, white, and pale purple.

- ☀ HEIGHT 2ft (60cm)
- ☀ SPREAD 1–1½ft (30–45cm)
- ☀ SITUATION Full sun
- ☀ SOIL Well-drained
- ☀ HARDINESS 30° to 20°F (-1° to -6°C)
- ☀ ZONES 3–8

## PRIMULA DENTICULATA
### HIMALAYAN PRIMULA
*Perennial*

A hardy border perennial, often grown as an annual or biennial to create color in spring-flowering displays in rock gardens and in moist soil alongside garden ponds. It develops compact, basal rosettes of pale green, somewhat spoon-shaped leaves. From early to late spring it reveals dense, globular heads packed with pale lilac to deep purple flowers.

There is also a white-flowered form of this perennial.

- ☀ HEIGHT 9–12in (23–30cm)
- ☀ SPREAD 8–10in (20–25cm)
- ☀ SITUATION Full sun or light shade
- ☀ SOIL Fertile and moisture-retentive
- ☀ HARDINESS -10° to -20°F (-23° to -28°C)
- ☀ ZONES 3–8

## SALVIA × SYLVESTRIS
### 'MAY NIGHT'
SALVIA × SYLVESTRIS 'MAINACHT'
*Herbaceous perennial*

A clump-forming border plant with oblong to lance-shaped, aromatic, mid- to dark green leaves and tall, narrow spires of violet-purple flowers from early summer to early fall.

'Purple Rain' develops rich purple flowers from midsummer to early fall on plants 45cm (1½ft) high.

❋ HEIGHT 1½ft (45cm)

❋ SPREAD 1¼–1½ft (38–45cm)

❋ SITUATION Full sun

❋ SOIL Fertile and well-drained

❋ HARDINESS -10° to -20°F
 (-23° to -28°C)

❋ ZONES 4–7

## STACHYS MACRANTHA
### 'SUPERBA'
WOOD BETONY
*Herbaceous perennial*

This border plant with upright stems is clump-forming and bears triangular to round, mid-green, and hairy leaves. From late spring to midsummer it develops clustered heads of rich rose-purple flowers.

There are several superb varieties, including 'Violacea', with violet-colored flowers, while 'Rosea' has rose flowers.

❋ HEIGHT 1½–2ft (45–60cm)

❋ SPREAD 1–1¼ft (30–38cm)

❋ SITUATION Full sun or partial shade

❋ SOIL Fertile and well-drained

❋ HARDINESS -10° to -20°F
 (-23° to -28°C)

❋ ZONES 4–7

## TRADESCANTIA ×
## ANDERSONIANA
### 'PURPLE DOME'
#### TRADESCANTIA VIRGINIANA
'PURPLE DOME'
TRINITY FLOWER
*Herbaceous perennial*

A distinctive border plant with dull-green, long, narrow, and pointed, straplike leaves. From early summer to early fall it develops small clusters of three-petalled, rich purple flowers.

There are several other superb varieties, extending the color range to white, violet-blue, light blue, and royal purple.

- ❊ **HEIGHT** 2ft (60cm)
- ❊ **SPREAD** 1¼–1½ft (38–45cm)
- ❊ **SITUATION** Full sun or partial shade
- ❊ **SOIL** Moisture-retentive but well-drained
- ❊ **HARDINESS** 10° to 0°F (-12° to -17°C)
- ❊ **ZONES** 4–9

## VERONICA SPICATA
SPIKE SPEEDWELL
*Herbaceous perennial*

An erect border plant with mid-green, oblong to lance-shaped, and tooth-edged leaves. From early to late summer it develops terminal clusters, 3–6in (7.5–15cm) long.

There are many varieties, in colors including purple, rose-pink, marine-blue, deep blue, rose-red, and deep pink.

- ❊ **HEIGHT** ½–1½ft (15–45cm)
- ❊ **SPREAD** 6–12in (15–30cm)
- ❊ **SITUATION** Full sun or partial shade
- ❊ **SOIL** Fertile, and moisture-retentive but well-drained
- ❊ **HARDINESS** -30° to -40°F (-34° to -40°C )
- ❊ **ZONES** 3–8

TRADESCANTIA × ANDERSONIANA 'PURPLE DOME'

## BUDDLEJA DAVIDII
### 'BLACK KNIGHT'
#### BUDDLEIA DAVIDII
#### 'BLACK KNIGHT'
##### BUTTERFLY BUSH
*Deciduous shrub*

A large shrub with an open, spreading habit and long, lance-shaped, dark green leaves. From midsummer to fall it bears long, tapering plumes, up to 20in (50cm) long, of very dark purple flowers that are sweetly scented.

There are several varieties, in colors including white, violet-blue, and lilac.

Regular pruning is essential; in early or mid-spring cut back all the previous year's shoots to 3in (7.5cm) of the old wood.

☀ **HEIGHT** 6–8ft (1.8–2.4m)

☀ **SPREAD** 6–8ft (1.8–2.4m)

☀ **SITUATION** Full sun

☀ **SOIL** Well-drained but moisture-retentive; it tolerates slightly chalky soil

☀ **HARDINESS** -10° to -20°F (-23° to -28°C)

☀ **ZONES** 5–9

## DABOECIA CANTABRICA
### IRISH HEATH
*Evergreen shrub*

A low-growing shrub with small, pointed, dark green leaves that display silvery undersides. From early summer to early winter it bears 6in (15cm) long clusters of rose-purple flowers.

There are several varieties, in colors including shades of purple, pink, and white.

Lightly clip off dead flowers in early spring.

☀ **HEIGHT** 2–3ft (60–90cm)

☀ **SPREAD** 2–3ft (60–90cm)

☀ **SITUATION** Full sun and an open position

☀ **SOIL** Slightly acid, and moisture-retentive but well-drained; it dislikes chalky soil

☀ **HARDINESS** 0° to -10°F (-17° to -23°C)

☀ **ZONES** 7–10

## FUCHSIA MAGELLANICA
MAGELLAN FUCHSIA
*Deciduous shrub*

A bushy and clump-forming, slightly tender shrub with upright stems bearing mid-green leaves and clusters of pendent, crimson and purple flowers from midsummer to early or mid-fall.

There are several varieties, in colors including pale pink, scarlet, and violet, and a variety with variegated leaves.

Prune in early spring by cutting all stems to ground level.

❋ HEIGHT 3–4ft (90cm–1.2m); sometimes more in warm regions
❋ SPREAD 2–3¼ft (60cm–1m)
❋ SITUATION Full sun or light shade, with shelter from cold wind and frost during late spring and early fall
❋ SOIL Fertile, and well-drained but moisture-retentive
❋ HARDINESS 0° to -10°F (-17° to -23°C)
❋ ZONES 8–10

## HEBE
'ALICIA AMHERST'
HEBE 'ROYAL PURPLE'
*Evergreen shrub*

A robust but slightly tender, small shrub with leathery, 3in (7.5cm) long, oblong, dark glossy-green leaves. It has deep purple-blue flowers borne in clusters 3in (7.5cm) or more long during late summer. Sometimes the flowers appear to be a rich, deep violet.

❋ HEIGHT 3–4ft (90cm–1.2m)
❋ SPREAD 4–5ft (1.2–1.5m)
❋ SITUATION Full sun and shelter from cold wind; do not plant in a frost pocket near the bottom of a slope
❋ SOIL Well-drained
❋ HARDINESS 10° to 0°F (-12° to -17°C)
❋ ZONES 8–10

## HIBISCUS SYRIACUS
### 'BLUE BIRD'
HIBISCUS SYRIACUS 'OISEAU BLEU'
SHRUB ALTHEA
*Deciduous shrub*

Bushy and upright, with rich green, three-lobed, and coarsely toothed leaves. From midsummer to early fall it bears 3in (7.5cm) wide, single, violet-blue flowers with darker eyes.

Other varieties extend the color range to white with red centers, wine-red, and rose-pink.

No regular pruning is needed, other than shortening long shoots immediately the shrub finishes flowering. Additionally, cut out frost-damaged shoot-tips in spring.

☀ HEIGHT 6–10ft (1.8–3m)

☀ SPREAD 4–6ft (1.2–1.8m)

☀ SITUATION Full sun or light shade, and shelter from cold wind

☀ SOIL Fertile, and well-drained but moisture-retentive

☀ HARDINESS -10° to -20°F (-23° to -28°C)

☀ ZONES 5–8

## INDIGOFERA HETERANTHA
### INDIGOFERA GERARDIANA
HIMALAYAN INDIGO
*Deciduous shrub*

A slightly tender, bushy, and well-branched shrub with leaves formed of many gray-green leaflets. The 3–5in (7.5–13cm) long clusters of rose-purple, pea-shaped flowers appear from midsummer to early fall.

No regular pruning is needed, other than cutting out dead or frosted shoots in spring. However, in cold areas, cut back all shoots to within 2–3in (5–7.5cm) of the soil.

When grown as a wall-shrub it grows higher and wider than when it is a freestanding shrub.

☀ HEIGHT 5–6ft (1.5–1.8m)

☀ SPREAD 4–5ft (1.2–1.5m)

☀ SITUATION Full sun and shelter from cold wind

☀ SOIL Moderately rich, and well-drained but moisture-retentive

☀ HARDINESS 10° to 0°F (-12° to -17°C)

☀ ZONES 4–7

## LEYCESTERIA FORMOSA
FORMOSA HONEYSUCKLE
*Deciduous shrub*

A distinctive shrub with upright,
hollow stems and somewhat long
and heart-shaped, glaucous, mid-
green leaves with tapering points.
During mid- and late summer it
develops white flowers surrounded
by claret-colored bracts.

Later, in mid-fall, this shrub
develops reddish-purple,
gooseberrylike fruits.

In mid-spring cut out at ground
level all shoots that bore flowers
the previous year.

* HEIGHT 5–6ft (1.5–1.8m)
* SPREAD 4–5ft (1.2–1.5m)
* SITUATION Full sun or light shade
* SOIL Well-drained
* HARDINESS 10° to 0°F
  (-12° to -17°C)
* ZONES 4–7

## RHODODENDRON
'PURPLE SPLENDOR'
*Evergreen shrub*

This hardy hybrid has a sturdy,
erect, bushy, and leafy nature.
During late spring and early
summer it develops large, dome-
shaped flower trusses packed with
up to 20 separate flowers. These are
funnel-shaped, deep purple with a
flare of black markings, and are up
to 3in (7.5cm) wide.

* HEIGHT 8–12ft (2.4–3.6m)
* SPREAD 8–12ft (2.4–3.6m)
* SITUATION Light shade and sheltered
  from cold wind
* SOIL Slightly acid, and well-drained but
  moisture-retentive
* HARDINESS 20° to 10°F
  (-6° to -12°C)
* ZONES 5–7

## ROSA
### 'ROSERAIE DE L'HAŸ'
#### ROSA RUGOSA
#### 'ROSERAIE DE L'HAŸ'
ROSE
*Deciduous shrub*

A well-known rose with bushy stems packed with prickles, and apple-green, glossy leaves that turn an attractive yellow in fall. During early summer, and often intermittently through to fall, it bears clusters of single, rich crimson-purple flowers, each 4in (10cm) or more wide. Additionally, it has creamy stamens.

❋ HEIGHT 5–7ft (1.5–2.1m)

❋ SPREAD 4–5ft (1.2–1.5m)

❋ SITUATION Full sun and an open position

❋ SOIL Well-drained but moisture-retentive

❋ HARDINESS -40° to -50°F (-40° to -45°C)

❋ ZONES 2–9

## SYRINGA VULGARIS
### 'CHARLES JOLY'
COMMON LILAC
*Deciduous shrub or small tree*

A familiar shrub or small tree with somewhat heart-shaped leaves and large, pyramidal heads packed with double, dark reddish-purple flowers that pale to a whitened plum-purple during early summer.

There are many single- and double-flowered varieties, extending the color range to white, lavender, lilac-blue, carmine-rose, and claret-red.

No regular pruning is needed, other than cutting off dead and faded flowers.

❋ HEIGHT 8–12ft (2.4–3.6m)

❋ SPREAD 6–10ft (1.8–3m)

❋ SITUATION Full sun or partial shade

❋ SOIL Fertile and well-drained

❋ HARDINESS -10° to -20°F (-23° to -28°C)

❋ ZONES 3–7

## AKEBIA QUINATA
FIVELEAF AKEBIA
*Semievergreen climber*

A twining climber, deciduous in
cold areas but evergreen in warm
regions, with leaves usually formed
of five leaflets, although sometimes
just three or four. During spring it
develops spicily scented, dark
chocolate-purple flowers. These
are followed by sausagelike,
purple or grayish-violet fruits.

No regular pruning is needed,
other than trimming back
excessively large plants in spring.

☀ HEIGHT 20–30ft (6–9m) when
   allowed to climb into trees
☀ SPREAD 12–15ft (3.6–4.5m) when
   allowed to climb into trees
☀ SITUATION Mild and warm
☀ SOIL Deeply prepared, fertile, and
   moisture-retentive but well-drained
☀ HARDINESS -10° to -20°F
   (-23° to -28°C)
☀ ZONES 4–8

## CLEMATIS VITICELLA
*Deciduous climber*

A popular, partially woody, and
slightly bushy climber with slender
stems and dark green leaves formed
of several leaflets. From midsummer
to early fall it bears purple-red or
violet, bell-shaped and nodding
flowers. Each flower is about
2–2½in (5–6.5cm) wide.

This climber dies back in winter,
and in early spring the plant is best
cut back to 1½–2ft (45–60cm)
above the ground.

☀ HEIGHT 8–12ft (2.4–3.6m)
☀ SPREAD 5–7ft (1.5–2.1m)
☀ SITUATION Full sun and an open
   position; ensure that the roots are
   shaded from strong sunlight
☀ SOIL Slightly alkaline, and well-drained
   but moisture-retentive
☀ HARDINESS 0° to -10°F
   (-17° to -23°C)
☀ ZONES 4–7

## SOLANUM CRISPUM
*Evergreen climber*

A bushy, scrambling, slightly tender climber that is semievergreen in cold areas. From early to late summer it bears clusters of purple-blue, star-shaped, 1in (2.5cm) wide flowers, which contain prominent yellow anthers.

It does not naturally cling to a wall and therefore a trellis is essential to support it.

❊ HEIGHT 6–15ft (1.8–4.5m)

❊ SPREAD 6–15ft (1.8–4.5m)

❊ SITUATION Full sun or light shade and, preferably, against a sunny, wind-sheltered wall

❊ SOIL Fertile, and moisture-retentive but well-drained

❊ HARDINESS 20° to 10°F (-6° to -12°C)

❊ ZONES 7–10

## WISTERIA FLORIBUNDA
### JAPANESE WISTERIA
*Deciduous climber*

A large climber with light to mid-green leaves, each formed of 12–19 leaflets. In fall these assume rich yellow tints. But this magnificent climber is mainly grown for its large, pendulous clusters of fragrant, violet-blue flowers, which appear during late spring and early summer.

There is also a white form.

❊ HEIGHT 25–30ft (7.5–9m)

❊ SPREAD 25–30ft (7.5–9m)

❊ SITUATION Full sun and shelter from cold wind; it grows well against a wall or on a pergola

❊ SOIL Fertile, and moisture-retentive but well-drained

❊ HARDINESS -10° to -20°F (-23° to -28°C)

❊ ZONES 4–9

## AJUGA REPTANS
### 'BRAUNHERZ'
CARPET BUGLE
*Herbaceous perennial*

## HEUCHERA MICRANTHA
### 'PALACE PURPLE'
ALUMROOT
*Herbaceous perennial*

A spreading, ground-covering plant with oblong to oval, shiny, and dark purple leaves. It develops erect shoots with whorls of blue flowers during early and midsummer.

*Ajuga reptans* 'Purpurescens' also has purple leaves tinted bronze, but the purple is not so intensive as it is in 'Braunherz'.

An eye-catching border plant with shallowly lobed, deep glossy, purple-bronze leaves. The stems are a similar color. Small, white, bell-like flowers appear in lax, spirelike clusters throughout the summer.

There are many other species, with flowers in colors that include white, rose-pink, blood-red, and scarlet.

- ☀ HEIGHT 6–12in (15–30cm)
- ☀ SPREAD 1–1¼ft (30–38cm)
- ☀ SITUATION Light shade
- ☀ SOIL Moisture-retentive
- ☀ HARDINESS 0° to -10°F (-17° to -23°C)
- ☀ ZONES 3–9

- ☀ HEIGHT 1½ft (45cm)
- ☀ SPREAD 1¼ft (38cm)
- ☀ SITUATION Full sun or partial shade
- ☀ SOIL Light and well-drained
- ☀ HARDINESS -10° to -20°F (-23° to -28°C)
- ☀ ZONES 4–8

HEUCHERA MICRANTHA 'PALACE PURPLE'

## OPHIOPOGON PLANISCAPUS
### 'NIGRESCENS'
BLACK-LEAVED LILY-TURF
*Herbaceous perennial*

A distinctive, creeping, and clump-forming border plant with long, narrow, and arching purple-black leaves. Additionally, it develops dense clusters of white flowers tinged with purple, on 6in (15cm) long stems during mid- and late summer. These are followed by purple-black berries.

- ❊ **HEIGHT** 8in (20cm)
- ❊ **SPREAD** 8–12in (20–30cm)
- ❊ **SITUATION** Full sun
- ❊ **SOIL** Well-drained but moisture-retentive
- ❊ **HARDINESS** 0° to -10°F (-17° to -23°C)
- ❊ **ZONES** 7–9

## PERILLA FRUTESCENS
### 'ATROPURPUREA LACINIATA'
*Semihardy annual*

A beautiful semihardy annual with oval, pointed, deeply toothed, and crumple-edged, spicily scented, deep reddish-purple leaves. During mid- and late summer, white flowers appear in 4in (10cm) long spikes. It is ideal for planting in summer-flowering bedding displays.

The variety *nankinensis* has deeply indented, finely cut bronze-purple leaves.

- ❊ **HEIGHT** 1½ft (45cm)
- ❊ **SPREAD** 1ft (30cm)
- ❊ **SITUATION** Full sun
- ❊ **SOIL** Well-drained
- ❊ **HARDINESS** Will not tolerate temperatures below 32°F (0°C)
- ❊ **ZONES** Tender, warm-season annual in zones 2–11

## BERBERIS THUNBERGII ATROPURPUREA
*Deciduous shrub*

A rounded and prickly shrub with small, somewhat pear-shaped, rich purple-red leaves throughout summer. The color increases in intensity during fall and with the approach of winter.

The form 'Atropurpurea Nana' is smaller, with similarly colored leaves.

No regular pruning is needed, other than occasionally cutting out old stems in early spring.

* ☀ HEIGHT 4–5ft (1.2–1.5m)
* ☀ SPREAD 4–5ft (1.2–1.5m)
* ☀ SITUATION Full sun; shade diminishes the intensity of the color in the leaves
* ☀ SOIL Moderately fertile and well-drained
* ☀ HARDINESS -20° to -30°F (-28° to 34°C)
* ☀ ZONES 4–8

## CORYLUS MAXIMA
'PURPUREA'
PURPLE FILBERT
*Deciduous shrub*

A magnificent and robust shrub with large, rounded, and somewhat heart-shaped, rich purple leaves throughout summer. They are said to rival the purple-leaved beech in the intensity of their coloring.

No regular pruning is needed, other than occasionally thinning out congested growth.

* ☀ HEIGHT 6–10ft (1.8–3m)
* ☀ SPREAD 6–10ft (1.8–3m)
* ☀ SITUATION Full sun, with shelter from cold wind
* ☀ SOIL Well-drained
* ☀ HARDINESS -10° to -20°F (-23° to -28°C)
* ☀ ZONES 4–8

## PHORMIUM TENAX
### 'PURPUREUM'
PURPLE-LEAVED NEW ZEALAND FLAX
*Evergreen perennial*

This semihardy evergreen perennial bears large, leathery, erect, straplike, bronze–purple leaves with rigid points. They are about 4in (10cm) wide.

From midsummer through to fall it develops dull red flowers, each being about 2in (5cm) long, on branched stems.

❄ HEIGHT 5–6ft (1.5–1.8m)

❄ SPREAD 4–5ft (1.2–1.5m)

❄ SITUATION Full sun and shelter from cold wind

❄ SOIL Deeply prepared, and moisture-retentive but well-drained

❄ HARDINESS 20° to 10°F (-6° to -12°C)

❄ ZONES 7–10

## PRUNUS × CISTENA
PURPLE-LEAVED SAND CHERRY
*Deciduous shrub*

This relatively dwarf, ornamental plum develops small, oval leaves, that are crimson when young, becoming bronze-red. White flowers appear during late spring.

One of its parents is *Prunus cerasifera* 'Pissardii', a purple-leaved form of the cherry plum. This bushy tree bears dark red leaves when young, which soon turn a deep purple.

No regular pruning is needed, other than cutting out damaged or misplaced branches in late summer.

❄ HEIGHT 4–5ft (1.2–1.5m)

❄ SPREAD 4–5ft (1.2–1.5m)

❄ SITUATION Full sun

❄ SOIL Moist, but not too dry or wet; it grows well in slightly chalky soil

❄ HARDINESS -30° to -40°F (-34° to -40°C)

❄ ZONES 2–8

### ROSA GLAUCA
ROSA RUBRIFOLIA
REDLEAF ROSE
*Deciduous shrub*

An erect rose with reddish–violet stems. The leaves, formed of five or seven leaflets, are a beautiful coppery or glaucous purple, especially when the shrub is in full sunlight. Where the shrub is in shade they are grayish–green, with a mauve tinge.

Clear pink flowers, each of which is about 1⅜in (36mm) wide, appear in sparse clusters during the early summer.

No regular pruning is needed, other than occasionally thinning out shoots in spring.

❋ HEIGHT 7ft (2.1m)
❋ SPREAD 5ft (1.5m)
❋ SITUATION Full sun and an
   open position
❋ SOIL Well-drained
❋ HARDINESS -40° to -50°F
   (-40° to -45°C)
❋ ZONES 2–8

### SALVIA OFFICINALIS 'PURPURASCENS'
SALVIA OFFICINALIS 'PURPUREA'
PURPLE-LEAF GARDEN SAGE
*Evergreen shrub*

A relatively short-lived and slightly tender shrub, which in cold regions may become semievergreen. The wrinkle-surfaced, fragrant leaves and stems are an attractive soft purple color.

Additionally, it reveals spires of bluish-purple flowers during early and midsummer.

❋ HEIGHT 1½–2ft (45–60cm)
❋ SPREAD 1½–2ft (45–60cm)
❋ SITUATION Full sun or light shade;
   shelter from cold wind is beneficial
❋ SOIL Well-drained but moisture-
   retentive
❋ HARDINESS -10° to -20°F
   (-23° to -28°C)
❋ ZONES 4–8

### SAMBUCUS NIGRA
**'GUINCHO PURPLE'**
SAMBUCUS NIGRA 'PURPUREA'
PURPLE-LEAF EUROPEAN ELDER
*Deciduous shrub*

An attractive shrub with leaves formed of five to seven, sharply toothed, green leaflets, which are flushed purple when young. Additionally, it develops flattened heads of cream-colored, sweetly fragrant flowers during early summer. These are followed by bunches of shiny black fruits.

No regular pruning is needed.

❋ **HEIGHT** 8–12ft (2.4–3.6m)

❋ **SPREAD** 8–12ft (2.4–3.6m)

❋ **SITUATION** Full sun or partial shade

❋ **SOIL** Fertile, and moisture-retentive but well-drained

❋ **HARDINESS** -10° to -20°F (-23° to -28°C)

❋ **ZONES** 5–6

### WEIGELA FLORIDA
**'FOLIIS PURPUREIS'**
OLD-FASHIONED WEIGELA
*Deciduous shrub*

A bushy, compact, slow-growing shrub with arching branches bearing purple, finely wrinkled leaves. During early summer it bears clusters of foxglove-like, pale-pink flowers.

Regular pruning encourages the yearly production of flowers; immediately these fade, cut back a few old stems to ground level.

❋ **HEIGHT** 4–5ft (1.2–1.5m)

❋ **SPREAD** 4–5ft (1.2–1.5m)

❋ **SITUATION** Full sun

❋ **SOIL** Well-drained but moisture-retentive

❋ **HARDINESS** -10° to -20°F (-23° to -28°C)

❋ **ZONES** 4–8

*Purple flowers are complemented here by cream-and-green ornamental cabbages.*

# index for purple

*See the following pages for other plants with several varieties, including purple:*

TRADESCANTIA X ANDERSONIANA 'PURPLE DOME'

# BLUE

*"True blue" is a wonderful color*
*for the garden—the color of the*
*sky on a bright sunny day.*

# the color blue
# blue plants

*The striking blue-green leaves of* Hosta sieboldiana *are a wonderful example of the type of blue foliage available for the garden.*

In many books and catalogs the color blue has become lost in the wide range of purples, indigoes, and violets. However, there is a true blue color, which can be found in a number of beautiful plants. It is important to understand what is meant by "true blue," as many of the so-called blue plants are actually lavender or violet-colored. True blue has no red or yellow in it and is the color of the sky on a brilliant summer's day. It is seen in the wonderful Himalayan poppy *Meconopsis betonicifolia*, in the English bluebell *Hyacinthoides non-scripta*, which carpets woods in spring, and in many hyacinths and delphiniums, as well as most of the gentians.

In foliage there is no true blue, as leaves always need to contain chlorophyll in order to function and this gives a green coloration to every leaf. However, in some foliage the green is overlaid with a blue film, which gives rise to wonderful glaucous-leaved plants (so-called after the Greek sea-god Glaucus), like *Hosta sieboldiana* and the stately *Melianthus major*.

There are even a few blue fruits, including the china-blue berries of *Tropaeolum speciosum*, which are great fun and worth seeking out to plant next to fall-coloring shrubs. There are also the dark blue fruits of blueberries themselves, *Vaccinium corymbosum*, although these are rather more satisfactory to grow for eating as fruit, rather than as part of a specific color combination.

MUSCARI ARMENIACUM

## COLOR HARMONIES

Blue, like yellow, is easy to use in the garden as it forms an adjacent color harmony with the green of most leaves. In spring much of the countryside is transformed into a harmony of yellow, blue, and green—primroses and speedwells or, in alpine meadows, cowslips and gentians. The opposite and contrasting color to blue is orange: this works superbly in the fall with late blue flowers and blue berries alongside the orange of fall foliage. The tints, tones, and shades of blue make a lovely planting combination, particularly when it includes plenty of the palest blue flowers, plus plants with glaucous foliage.

## USING BLUE IN YOUR GARDEN

Try planting bright blue flowers against plum and purple foliage for a stunning display. Equally effective is a blue and white planting: a white tulip among grape hyacinths; or white roses among blue delphiniums, campanulas, platycodons, and veronicas.

*Blue is easy to plant in the garden, as it harmonizes beautifully with purples, greens, and whites.*

### AGERATUM
### 'BLUE MINK'
#### AGERATUM HOUSTONIANUM
#### 'BLUE MINK'
##### AGERATUM
*Semihardy annual*

A superb dwarf and compact
semihardy annual, with mid-green,
heart-shaped, and hairy leaves.
From early summer through to
the frosts of fall it reveals large,
clustered heads of fluffy, powder-
blue flowers.

The range of varieties is wide
and encompasses colors such as
bright blue, mauve, and pink, as
well as white.

- ❋ HEIGHT 9–12in (23–30cm)
- ❋ SPREAD 8–10in (20–25cm)
- ❋ SITUATION Full sun and shelter
  from cold wind
- ❋ SOIL Moderately fertile and
  moisture-retentive
- ❋ HARDINESS Will not tolerate
  temperatures below 32°F (0°C)
- ❋ ZONES Semihardy, warm-season
  annual in zones 2–11

### BRACHYSCOME IBERIDIFOLIA
### 'BLUE STAR'
#### SWAN RIVER DAISY
*Semihardy annual*

A distinctive plant, with deeply cut,
pale-green leaves on slender stems.
From early summer to early fall it
bears large, cineraria-like, rich blue
flowers, each with a golden, slightly
raised cone at its center.

The range of varieties is wide and
encompasses pink, lilac, mauve, and
purple-blue, as well as white.

- ❋ HEIGHT 9–12in (23–30cm)
- ❋ SPREAD 8–10in (20–25cm)
- ❋ SITUATION Full sun and shelter
  from cold, blustery wind
- ❋ SOIL Fertile, and moisture-retentive
  but well-drained
- ❋ HARDINESS Will not tolerate
  temperatures below 32°F (0°C)
- ❋ ZONES Cool-season annual in
  zones 2–11

## CENTAUREA CYANUS 'BLUE DIADEM'
BACHELOR'S-BUTTON
*Hardy annual*

A popular annual with a cottage-garden nature. The narrowly lance-shaped, gray-green leaves are surmounted from early summer to early fall with branched sprays of double, powder-puff blue, 2⅖in (6cm) wide flowers.

- ☀ **HEIGHT** 2½ft (75cm)
- ☀ **SPREAD** 1¼ft (38cm)
- ☀ **SITUATION** Full sun
- ☀ **SOIL** Fertile and well-drained
- ☀ **HARDINESS** Tolerates slight frost
- ☀ **ZONES** Biennial, grown as warm-season annual in zones 2–8; as cool-season annual in zones 9–11

## LOBELIA 'CAMBRIDGE BLUE'
LOBELIA ERINUS 'CAMBRIDGE BLUE'
*Semihardy annual*

This floriferous semihardy perennial is usually grown as a semihardy annual. From late spring to the frosts of fall it bears masses of clear sky-blue flowers.

The range of varieties is wide and encompasses white and many shades of blue.

As well as compact varieties for filling border edges and troughs with color, there are trailing types for planting in hanging-baskets.

- ☀ **HEIGHT** 4–6in (10–15cm)
- ☀ **SPREAD** 8–12in (20–30cm)
- ☀ **SITUATION** Partial shade
- ☀ **SOIL** Fertile, and moisture-retentive but well-drained
- ☀ **HARDINESS** Will not tolerate temperatures below 32°F (0°C)
- ☀ **ZONES** Tender perennial, grown as a cool-season annual in zones 2–11

LOBELIA 'CAMBRIDGE BLUE'

**annuals** 167

## MYOSOTIS
### 'ROYAL BLUE'
MYOSOTIS SYLVATICA
'ROYAL BLUE'
FORGET-ME-NOT
*Biennial*

A widely grown, bushy biennial with mid-green and hairy, spoon-shaped leaves. During late spring and early summer it develops deep blue flowers, borne in clustered, terminal heads.

The range of varieties and colors is wide and—as well as many shades of blue—includes pink; it is also sold in color mixtures of white, blue, rose, and pink.

❊ HEIGHT 9–12in (23–30cm)

❊ SPREAD 6–8in (15–20cm)

❊ SITUATION Partial shade

❊ SOIL Fertile and moisture-retentive; dry soil tends to cause plants to die during winter

❊ HARDINESS Tolerates temperatures down to about 20°F (-6°C)

❊ ZONES Biennial in zones 3–8

## NEMOPHILA MENZIESII
NEMOPHILA INSIGNIS
BABY-BLUE-EYES
*Hardy annual*

A petite and enchanting hardy annual for edging borders. It has a slightly spreading and bushy habit, with feathery, light green leaves. Sky-blue, buttercup-shaped flowers, about 1½in (36mm) wide and with white centers, appear from early to late summer.

❊ HEIGHT 9in (23cm)

❊ SPREAD 6in (15cm)

❊ SITUATION Full sun or partial shade

❊ SOIL Light, cool, fertile, and moisture-retentive

❊ HARDINESS Tolerates slight frost

❊ ZONES Hardy, cool-season annual in zones 2–11

## NIGELLA DAMASCENA
'MISS JEKYLL'
LOVE-IN-A-MIST
*Hardy annual*

A distinctive hardy annual, well known for its bright green, fernlike leaves, which create an attractive foil for the large, semidouble, bright blue flowers, each about 1½in (36mm) wide, from early to late summer.

There are many varieties, extending the color range from blue to mauve, rose-pink, purple, and white.

※ HEIGHT 1½–2ft (45–60cm)
※ SPREAD 10–12in (25–30cm)
※ SITUATION Full sun
※ SOIL Well-drained
※ HARDINESS Tolerates slight frost
※ ZONES Hardy, cool-season annual in zones 2–11

## NOLANA PARADOXA
'BLUE BIRD'
*Semihardy annual*

A tender perennial invariably grown as a semihardy annual. It is ideal for planting in borders, window boxes, and hanging-baskets. It has succulent, creeping stems that bear a profusion of 2in (5cm) wide, trumpet-shaped, sky-blue flowers with cream-colored throats.

※ HEIGHT 6–8in (15–20cm)
※ SPREAD 8–10in (20–25cm)
※ SITUATION Full sun
※ SOIL Moisture-retentive but well-drained
※ HARDINESS Will not tolerate temperatures below 32°F (0°C)
※ ZONES Semihardy, warm-season annual in zones 2–11

## CHIONODOXA LUCILIAE
GLORY-OF-THE-SNOW
*Bulb*

A diminutive bulbous plant, ideal for planting in a rock garden or sink garden, at the front of a border or for naturalizing in short grass. It has mid-green, narrow, and strap-like, blunt-tipped leaves.

Six-petalled, star-shaped, light blue flowers with white centers appear during late winter and early spring.

There is also a white-flowered form of this plant.

Plant the bulbs 2–3in (5–7.5cm) deep, in small clusters.

❉ HEIGHT 4in (10cm)

❉ SPREAD Space bulbs 3in (7.5cm) apart

❉ SITUATION Full sun

❉ SOIL Well-drained

❉ HARDINESS -20° to -30°F
    (-28° to -34°C)

❉ ZONES 4–9

## HYACINTHOIDES NON-SCRIPTA
ENDYMION NONSCRIPTUS
ENGLISH BLUEBELL
*Bulb*

This beautiful bulbous plant, also commonly known as wild hyacinth and botanically sometimes listed as *Scilla non-scripta*, bears nodding, bell-shaped, purple-blue flowers during late spring and early summer. It is an ideal plant for naturalizing under deciduous trees in a wild garden.

Plant the bulbs 4–6in (10–15cm) deep in late summer or fall, as soon as they are available. Do not allow them to become dry while waiting to be planted.

❉ HEIGHT 10–12in (25–30cm)

❉ SPREAD Space bulbs 4in (10cm) apart

❉ SITUATION Dappled light

❉ SOIL Fertile, and moisture retentive but well-drained

❉ HARDINESS -10° to -20°F
    (-23° to -28°C)

❉ ZONES 4–8

## HYACINTHUS ORIENTALIS 'BLUE JACKET'
COMMON HYACINTH
*Bulb*

A well-known bulb, with upright, soldierlike spires packed with bell-shaped, navy flowers striped with purple during late spring.

Plant the bulbs 5–6in (13–15cm) deep in early fall to create color in spring-flowering displays. After the flowers fade, dig up the bulbs so that summer-flowering plants can be put in their place.

Other varieties extend the color range to white, yellow, red, and pink.

❋ HEIGHT 6–9in (15–23cm)

❋ SPREAD Space bulbs 6–8in (15–20cm) apart

❋ SITUATION Full sun

❋ SOIL Moderately fertile, and moisture-retentive but well-drained

❋ HARDINESS 20° to 10°F (-6° to -12°C)

❋ ZONES 3–7

## MUSCARI ARMENIACUM
ARMENIAN GRAPE-HYACINTH
*Bulb*

A popular bulbous plant for rock gardens and the fronts of borders. It develops narrow, mid-green, and spreading, straplike leaves. These create an attractive foil for the densely packed, deep blue flowers with white rims, which appear during mid- and late spring.

There are several varieties, with flowers in white as well as shades of blue.

Plant the bulbs 3in (7.5cm) deep during late summer and early fall.

❋ HEIGHT 8in (20cm)

❋ SPREAD Space bulbs 3–4in (7.5–10cm) apart

❋ SITUATION Full sun; shade decreases the display and increases the amount of leaf growth

❋ SOIL Well-drained

❋ HARDINESS -20° to -30°F (-28° to -34°C)

❋ ZONES 2–8

## SCILLA SIBERICA
SIBERIAN SQUILL
*Bulb*

This bulbous plant is ideal for planting in rock gardens, as well as for naturalizing in short grass. The glossy green, straplike leaves appear in early spring, with the brilliant blue, bell-shaped flowers breaking into color in mid-spring.

Plant the bulbs 2–3in (5–7.5cm) deep in either late summer or early fall.

❊ HEIGHT 4–6in (10–15cm)

❊ SPREAD Space bulbs 3in (7.5cm) apart

❊ SITUATION Full sun or partial shade

❊ SOIL Moisture-retentive but well-drained

❊ HARDINESS -10° to -20°F (-23° to -28°C)

❊ ZONES 2–8

## AGAPANTHUS CAMPANULATUS
AFRICAN LILY
*Deciduous perennial*

An almost hardy, deciduous, clump-forming border perennial with fleshy roots and mid-green, strap-like leaves that arise from the plant's base. During late summer it develops pale-blue flowers carried on long stems in inverted umbrellalike heads.

The variety called 'Isis' has deep Pacific-blue flowers during mid- and late summer.

❊ HEIGHT 2–2½ft (60–75cm)

❊ SPREAD 1½ft (45cm)

❊ SITUATION Full sun

❊ SOIL Fertile, and moisture-retentive but well-drained

❊ HARDINESS 10° to 0°F (-12° to -17°C)

❊ ZONES 8–12; mulch in zone 7

## ANCHUSA AZUREA
### 'LODDON ROYALIST'
ANCHUSA ITALICA
'LODDON ROYALIST'
ITALIAN BUGLOSS
*Herbaceous perennial*

A widely grown, clump-forming border plant with mid-green, lance-shaped leaves and tall, lax spires of salver-shaped, gentian-blue flowers from early to late summer. Sometimes, but only in mild areas, it continues flowering into the early days of early fall.

There are several other attractive blue varieties.

It is a very reliable border plant and one that is widely grown in herbaceous borders.

☼ **HEIGHT** 3ft (90cm)

☼ **SPREAD** 1¼–1½ft (38–45cm)

☼ **SITUATION** Full sun

☼ **SOIL** Fertile, and well-drained but moisture-retentive

☼ **HARDINESS** -30° to -40°F (-34° to -40°C)

☼ **ZONES** 3–8

## AQUILEGIA VULGARIS
EUROPEAN COLUMBINE
*Herbaceous perennial*

A well-known, cottage-garden plant with gray-green leaves that have the appearance of a large maidenhair fern. From late spring to midsummer it develops distinctive blue and white flowers with long spurs.

There are many varieties, in colors including shades of pink, red, cream, blue, pink, yellow, and white.

☼ **HEIGHT** 1½–1¾ft (45–50cm)

☼ **SPREAD** 1–1¼ft (30–38cm)

☼ **SITUATION** Full sun or partial shade

☼ **SOIL** Moisture-retentive but well-drained

☼ **HARDINESS** -20° to -30°F (-28° to -34°C)

☼ **ZONES** 3–8

## ASTER NOVI-BELGII
### 'MARIE BALLARD'
NEW YORK DAISY
*Herbaceous perennial*

A popular border plant with
slender-pointed and stem-clasping,
mid- to deep green leaves. During
early and mid-fall it develops large,
2in (5cm) wide, daisylike, light
blue, double flowers.

The range of varieties is wide and
includes colors such as creamy
white, pink, violet-blue, carmine,
and rosy red.

- ☀ HEIGHT 2½–3ft (75–90cm)
- ☀ SPREAD 1¼–1½ft (38–45cm)
- ☀ SITUATION Full sun
- ☀ SOIL Fertile, and moisture-retentive
  but well-drained
- ☀ HARDINESS -40° to -50°F
  (-40° to -45°C)
- ☀ ZONES 4–8

## CAMPANULA PERSICIFOLIA
### 'TELHAM BEAUTY'
PEACH-LEAVED BELLFLOWER
*Evergreen perennial*

A superb border plant with an
evergreen nature. It develops a basal
rosette of dark green, narrow, and
leathery leaves. Upright stems bear
clusters of 1in (2.5cm) wide,
saucer-shaped, rich-blue flowers
from early to late summer. Remove
dead flowers to encourage the
development of further flowers.

As well as blue forms, there is a
white variety.

- ☀ HEIGHT 1½–2ft (45–60cm)
- ☀ SPREAD 1–1¼ft (30–38cm)
- ☀ SITUATION Full sun or partial shade
- ☀ SOIL Fertile and well-drained
- ☀ HARDINESS -30° to -40°F
  (-34° to -40°C)
- ☀ ZONES 3–6

## CLEMATIS HERACLEIFOLIA
TUBE CLEMATIS
*Herbaceous perennial*

This unusual clematis has an herbaceous nature with a slightly woody base. In mild areas it often forms a sprawling subshrub. It develops coarsely toothed, dark green leaves with a downy nature. During late summer and into early fall it bears clusters of small, tubular, purple-blue flowers.

The form *C. heracleifolia davidiana* 'Wyevale' displays fragrant, flax-blue flowers.

※ HEIGHT 2–3ft (60–90cm)

※ SPREAD 1½–2ft (45–60cm)

※ SITUATION Full sun

※ SOIL Well-drained but moisture-retentive, and slightly alkaline

※ HARDINESS -30° to -40°F (-34° to -40°C)

※ ZONES 3–8

## CORYDALIS FLEXUOSA
'CHINA BLUE'
*Tuber*

An exotic-looking tuberous plant that is ideal for planting at the edge of a narrow border or in a rock garden. It reveals luxurious, deeply cut, deep green leaves, topped from late spring to midsummer with numerous sky-blue flowers borne on slender stems. Incidentally, the early foliage and buds are slightly pink-tinged.

※ HEIGHT 6–8in (15–20cm)

※ SPREAD 6–8in (15–20cm), but usually forms a large clump eventually

※ SITUATION Full sun or partial shade

※ SOIL Well-drained, light, and cool; it does not like lime in the soil

※ HARDINESS 10° to 0°F (-12° to -17°C)

※ ZONES 5–8

## DELPHINIUM
### 'BLUE JAY'
DELPHINIUM ELATUM 'BLUE JAY'
CANDLE LARKSPUR
*Herbaceous perennial*

This *Elatum* variety creates tall, dominant spires of mid-blue, cup-shaped flowers with white eyes during the latter part of early summer and into midsummer.

It is an erect border plant, with mid-green, toothed, and deeply cut leaves.

The range of varieties is wide and includes mainly blue-colored flowers, but also pure-white, silvery mauve, and light purple.

* HEIGHT 5–6ft (1.5–1.8m)
* SPREAD 1½–2ft (45–60cm)
* SITUATION Full sun and sheltered from strong, blustery wind
* SOIL Fertile, moisture-retentive but well-drained
* HARDINESS -30° to -40°F (-34° to -40°C)
* ZONES 2–7

## GENTIANA ACAULIS
STEMLESS GENTIAN
*Hardy perennial*

A diminutive gentian that is ideal for planting in rock gardens. It creates a wealth of large, upright, blue, trumpetlike, 2–3in (5–7.5cm) long flowers. These appear above spreading mats of evergreen, glossy, mid-green leaves during late spring and early summer.

* HEIGHT 3–4in (7.5–10cm)
* SPREAD 1¼–1½ft (38–45cm)
* SITUATION Full sun
* SOIL Well-drained and slightly alkaline
* HARDINESS -30° to -40°F (-34° to -40°C)
* ZONES 4–7

## GERANIUM WALLICHIANUM
### 'BUXTON'S VARIETY'
GERANIUM WALLICHIANUM
'BUXTON'S BLUE'
WALLICH GERANIUM
*Herbaceous perennial*

A low-growing, dense, and compact border geranium with light green, silky and shiny, wedge-shaped, and deeply toothed leaves. From midsummer to early fall it develops clear-blue flowers with white centers. Each flower is about 1⅖in (36mm) wide.

This is an ideal geranium either for a large rock garden or the front of a border.

☀ HEIGHT 6–9in (15–23cm)

☀ SPREAD 2ft (60cm)

☀ SITUATION Full sun or partial shade

☀ SOIL Well-drained

☀ HARDINESS 10° to 0°F
  (-12° to -17°C)

☀ ZONES 3–8

## IRIS
### 'JANE PHILLIPS'
IRIS GERMANICA 'JANE PHILLIPS'
GERMAN IRIS
*Evergreen perennial*

Also known as flag iris and June iris, this superb rhizomatous-rooted hybrid iris has long, swordlike, mid-green leaves that last throughout the year. During early summer this variety develops large flowers, up to 5in (13cm) wide, formed of ruffled flax-blue petals.

There is an extensive range of these hybrid bearded irises, in a wide medley of colors.

☀ HEIGHT 2½ft (75cm)

☀ SPREAD 1¼–1½ft (38–45cm)

☀ SITUATION Full sun and shelter from strong, blustery wind

☀ SOIL Fertile, and well-drained but moisture-retentive

☀ HARDINESS 20° to 10°F
  (-6° to -12°C)

☀ ZONES 3–10

☀ ⬚ ░ ⫸ ✿ ⚶

## LINUM PERENNE
PERENNIAL FLAX
*Perennial border plant*

An erect, relatively short-lived, well-branched border plant with gray-green, narrow, and lance-shaped leaves. From early to late summer it bears 1in (2.5cm) wide, salver-shaped, sky-blue flowers.

It is a plant that is easily raised from seed.

❋ HEIGHT 1–1½ft (30–45cm)

❋ SPREAD 1ft (30cm)

❋ SITUATION Full sun

❋ SOIL Well-drained

❋ HARDINESS 10° to 0°F
(-12° to -17°C)

❋ ZONES 4–9

☀ ◐ ░ ⫸ ✿ ⚶

## MECONOPSIS BETONICIFOLIA
MECONOPSIS BAILEYI
BLUE-POPPY
*Herbaceous perennial*

A beautiful plant, with a clump-forming nature and long, mid-green leaves that taper to a blunt point. During early and midsummer it develops long, stiff, and upright stems that bear sky-blue, 3in (7.5cm) wide flowers with yellow anthers.

It is a short-lived perennial, but by cutting off the flowering stems before they bear flowers during the first year the plant's eventual life can be extended.

❋ HEIGHT 3–5ft (90cm–1.5m)

❋ SPREAD 1–1½ft (30–45cm)

❋ SITUATION Semishaded,
cool, and sheltered from
cold wind

❋ SOIL Fertile, lime-free, and
moisture-retentive but
well-drained

❋ HARDINESS 10° to 0°F
(-12° to -17°C)

❋ ZONES 4–7

LINUM PERENNE

## PHLOX STOLONIFERA
### 'BLUE RIDGE'
CREEPING PHLOX
*Herbaceous perennial*

A creeping perennial, forming a mat of long-stemmed, glossy, spoon- to pear-shaped leaves about 3in (7.5cm) long. During early and midsummer it bears blue, 1in (2.5cm) wide flowers.

There are many other varieties, in colors including violet, lavender, purple, and lilac, as well as white.

☼ HEIGHT 6–10in (15–25cm)
☼ SPREAD 10–12in (25–30cm) or more
☼ SITUATION Full sun or partial shade
☼ SOIL Fertile, and well-drained but moisture-retentive
☼ HARDINESS -20° to -30°F (-28° to -34°C)
☼ ZONES 2–8

## PLATYCODON GRANDIFLORUS
BALLOONFLOWER
*Herbaceous perennial*

A popular, long-lived, and clump-forming border plant with broad, glaucous leaves and upward stems bearing light blue, saucer-shaped flowers, each about 1½in (36mm) wide and in terminal clusters, from early to late summer.

There are several varieties, with blue, white or pink flowers.

This plant gains its common name from the balloon-like nature of its buds.

☼ HEIGHT 1½–2ft (45–60cm)
☼ SPREAD 1¼ft (38cm)
☼ SITUATION Full sun
☼ SOIL Well-drained
☼ HARDINESS -20° to -30°F (-28° to -34°C )
☼ ZONES 3–8

## SCABIOSA
### 'BUTTERFLY BLUE'
SCABIOSA CAUCASICA
'BUTTERFLY BLUE'
CAUCASIAN SCABIOUS
*Herbaceous perennial*

A distinctive and trouble-free border plant, forming low clusters of mid-green, lance-shaped leaves; the upper part of each leaf is formed of narrow segments. From early summer through to early fall it produces masses of intense lavender-blue, pincushion-like heads.

The flower heads are ideal for cutting, drying, and displaying in flower arrangements indoors.

※ HEIGHT 8–15in (20–38cm)

※ SPREAD 1–1¼ft (30–38cm)

※ SITUATION Full sun

※ SOIL Fertile and well-drained

※ HARDINESS -20° to -30°F
   (-28° to -34°C)

※ ZONES 3–7

## VERONICA AUSTRIACA
## TEUCRIUM
### 'CRATER LAKE BLUE'
VERONICA TEUCRIUM
'CRATER LAKE BLUE'
*Herbaceous perennial*

A clump-forming border plant with slender-pointed, narrowly lance-shaped, mid-green leaves. From early to late summer tall stems bear narrow, tapering heads of ultramarine blue flowers.

There are several other varieties, mainly in blue, but also in shades of pink. There is also a white-flowered form.

※ HEIGHT 1¼ft (38cm)

※ SPREAD 9–12in (23–30cm)

※ SITUATION Full sun or partial shade

※ SOIL Well-drained

※ HARDINESS 0° to -10°F
   (-17° to -23°C)

※ ZONES 4–8

## CEANOTHUS IMPRESSUS
SANTA BARBARA CEANOTHUS
*Evergreen shrub*

This bushy and densely branched, semihardy shrub is usually grown in the shelter of a wall. It has small, dark green, glossy leaves with downy undersides. In late spring it reveals small, deep blue flowers in clusters about 1in (2.5cm) long.

There are several other blue-flowered evergreen or deciduous species of this shrub.

- ❉ HEIGHT 6–10ft (1.8–3m) when planted in the shelter of a warm wall
- ❉ SPREAD 5–7ft (1.5–2.1m)
- ❉ SITUATION Full sun and shelter from cold wind
- ❉ SOIL Well-drained but moisture-retentive; avoid chalky soil
- ❉ HARDINESS 10° to 0°F (-12° to -17°C)
- ❉ ZONES 6–8

## CERATOSTIGMA WILLMOTIANUM
WILLMOTT BLUE LEADWORT
*Deciduous shrub*

This popular half-hardy shrub creates a mass of dark-green, diamond-shaped, and stalkless leaves, which in fall assume rich red and purple tints. From midsummer to the frosts of fall it creates clusters of small, rich cobalt-blue flowers.

In spring cut out all old and damaged shoots to ground level. In cold areas this may mean cutting down the entire plant.

- ❉ HEIGHT 2–3ft (60–90cm)
- ❉ SPREAD 2–3ft (60–90cm)
- ❉ SITUATION Full sun and sheltered from cold wind
- ❉ SOIL Well-drained
- ❉ HARDINESS 10° to 0°F (-12° to -17°C)
- ❉ ZONES 7–10

## HYDRANGEA MACROPHYLLA
### 'BLUE WAVE'
HYDRANGEA MACROPHYLLA
'MARIESII PERFECTA'
HOUSE HYDRANGEA
*Deciduous shrub*

A rounded shrub with a wealth of oval to lance-shaped, mid-green leaves, assuming purple and red tints in fall. From midsummer to early fall it reveals large, 4–6in (10–15cm) wide, flattened heads of blue flowers, surrounded by pink to blue ray florets.

Little pruning is needed, other than cutting out a few old stems at ground level in spring, and dead flower heads in fall or spring.

- ☀ HEIGHT 5–6ft (1.5–1.8m); more in warm areas
- ☀ SPREAD 5–6ft (1.5–1.8m); more in warm areas
- ☀ SITUATION Dappled light
- ☀ SOIL Slightly acid, and moisture-retentive but well-drained
- ☀ HARDINESS -10° to -20°F (-23° to -28°C)
- ☀ ZONES 6–9

## HYSSOPUS OFFICINALIS
HYSSOP
*Subshrubby perennial*

In warm regions this Asian and Mediterranean plant has a soft-stemmed and woody-base nature, but in cooler and temperate areas it becomes herbaceous, with all stems dying down to soil level in early winter.

The erect stems are clustered with aromatic, mid-green leaves, with tubular and lipped, purple-blue flowers appearing from mid-summer to early fall.

There is a white-flowered form, as well as one with pink flowers.

- ☀ HEIGHT 1½ft (45cm); more in warm areas
- ☀ SPREAD 1¼–1½ft (38–45cm); more in warm areas
- ☀ SITUATION Full sun and sheltered from cold wind
- ☀ SOIL Well-drained
- ☀ HARDINESS -30° to -40°F (-34° to -40°C)
- ☀ ZONES 3–9

## RHODODENDRON AUGUSTINII
*Evergreen shrub or small tree*

A superb, erect, and bushy shrub or small tree, vigorous in the wild, but moderate in cultivation. The oblong to lance-shaped, dark green leaves, up to 4in (10cm) long, have scaly undersides. During mid- and late spring it bears funnel-shaped, 2⅓in (6cm) wide flowers that range in color from mauve to dark blue. Each flower has a green-spotted throat.

It is slightly tender, and plants with dark blue flowers are the least hardy.

☀ HEIGHT 5–10ft (1.5–3m)

☀ SPREAD 5–6ft (1.5–1.8m)

☀ SITUATION Dappled light or semishade

☀ SOIL Fertile, slightly acid, and moisture-retentive but well-drained

☀ HARDINESS 0° to -10°F (-17° to -23°C)

☀ ZONES 6–8

## VINCA MINOR
PERIWINKLE
*Evergreen trailing shrub*

A well-known sprawling and trailing, low-growing shrub. From mid-spring to midsummer its many stems are peppered with blue flowers, each up to 1in (2.5cm) across. Sometimes flowering continues intermittently until the fall.

There are several varieties, with flowers in white, wine-red, and deep blue-purple, as well as shades of blue.

No regular pruning is needed, other than cutting back excessively large plants in spring.

☀ HEIGHT 4–6in (10–15cm)

☀ SPREAD 3–4ft (90cm–1.2m)

☀ SITUATION Partial shade

☀ SOIL Well-drained

☀ HARDINESS -20° to -30°F (-28° to -34°C)

☀ ZONES 3–8

## CLEMATIS ALPINA
ALPINE CLEMATIS
*Deciduous climber*

A dainty, bushy, rather weak-growing climber with dark green leaves formed of nine coarsely toothed leaflets. During spring, and sometimes into early summer, it develops masses of pendulous, nodding, cup-shaped, violet-blue flowers, each of which is about 1½in (36mm) wide.

No regular pruning is needed, other than lightly cutting back excessively large plants soon after their flowers fade.

- ❋ HEIGHT 6–8ft (1.8–2.4m)
- ❋ SPREAD 4–5ft (1.2–1.5m)
- ❋ SITUATION Full sun and an open position, but the roots must be shaded from direct and strong sunlight
- ❋ SOIL Well-drained but moisture-retentive, and slightly alkaline
- ❋ HARDINESS -10° to -20°F (-23° to -28°C)
- ❋ ZONES 4–7

## CLEMATIS 'PERLE D'AZURE'
LARGE-FLOWERED CLEMATIS
*Deciduous climber*

A vigorous climber with mid-green leaves of three or five leaflets. From midsummer to fall it bears 2½in (6cm) wide, light blue flowers with a pinkish-mauve flush.

In early spring cut all shoots back to just above a pair of strong buds, 2½ft (75cm) above the ground.

- ❋ HEIGHT 10–12ft (3–3.6m)
- ❋ SPREAD 5–6ft (1.5–1.8m)
- ❋ SITUATION Full sun and an open position; ensure the roots are shaded
- ❋ SOIL Slightly chalky, and well-drained but moisture-retentive
- ❋ HARDINESS 0° to -10°F (-17° to -23°C)
- ❋ ZONES 3–8

CLEMATIS 'PERLE D'AZURE'

## IPOMOEA TRICOLOR
### 'HEAVENLY BLUE'
MORNING-GLORY
*Annual climber*

This semihardy annual is well known and, despite having a perennial nature in warm countries, in temperate regions it benefits from gentle warmth early in its life. It is ideal for smothering trellises and chain-link fencing with a dense screen of large, sky-blue, trumpet-shaped flowers from midsummer to fall.

☀ HEIGHT 6–7ft (1.8–2.1m)

☀ SPREAD 3–4ft (90cm–1.2m)

☀ SITUATION Full sun and shelter from cold wind

☀ SOIL Fertile, light, and moisture-retentive but well-drained

☀ HARDINESS Tolerates slight frost

☀ ZONES Cool-season annual in zones 2–11

## LATHYRUS ODORATUS
SWEET PEA
*Annual climber*

A well-known annual climber with fragrant, 1in (2.5cm) wide, blue flowers, with elegantly waved petals. They are borne amid leaves formed of pairs of mid-green, oval leaflets.

Although this is a hardy annual, the seeds are usually sown in gentle warmth early in the year. Alternatively, seeds can be sown in spring, where they are to grow and flower.

There are many varieties of this sweet pea, in colors including shades of red, blue, pink, and purple, as well as white.

☀ HEIGHT 6–10ft (1.8–3m)

☀ SPREAD 2–4ft (60cm–1.2m)

☀ SITUATION Full sun

☀ SOIL Fertile, and moisture-retentive but well-drained; slightly alkaline soil suits it best

☀ HARDINESS Tolerates slight frost

☀ ZONES Hardy; cool-season annual in zones 2–11

## CLERODENDRON TRICHOTOMUM FARGESII

HARLEQUIN GLORY-BOWER

*Deciduous shrub*

A bushy shrub with a sparse habit and pithy branches bearing oval, dark green leaves up to 6in (15cm) long; they are tinged purple in fall. The leaves have an unpleasant odor when crushed.

During late summer and early fall it bears fragrant, star-shaped, pink and white flowers in clusters 6–9in (15–23cm) wide. These are followed by china-blue berries held in crimson calyces.

☀ HEIGHT 10–15ft (3–4.5m)

☀ SPREAD 10–15ft (3–4.5m)

☀ SITUATION Full sun and shelter from cold wind

☀ SOIL Fertile and well-drained

☀ HARDINESS 20° to 10°F (-6° to -12°C)

☀ ZONES 6–9

## CORNUS ALBA

DOGWOOD

*Deciduous shrub*

Slightly sprawling and suckering shrub with oval to wedge-shaped, mid-green leaves that often assume red and orange tints in fall. The upright, green stems become red in winter. Inconspicuous yellow-white flowers appear during late spring and early summer, and are followed by white, rounded berries, about the size of garden peas, which are tinted blue.

☀ HEIGHT 6–9ft (1.8–2.7m)

☀ SPREAD 6–9ft (1.8–2.7m)

☀ SITUATION Full sun or light shade

☀ SOIL Well-drained but moisture-retentive

☀ HARDINESS -30° to -40°F (-34° to -40°C)

☀ ZONES 2–7

## VACCINIUM CORYMBOSUM
HIGHBUSH BLUEBERRY
*Deciduous shrub*

A thicket-forming and erect, well-branched shrub with oval to lance-shaped, pointed, and mid-green leaves that assume rich red shades in fall. White, pink-tinted flowers appear during late spring and early summer; they are followed by round, blue-black, ½in (12mm) wide berries borne in tight clusters. The berries are covered with a waxy bloom.

- ☀ HEIGHT 4–6ft (1.2–1.8m)
- ☀ SPREAD 6–7ft (1.8–2.1m)
- ☀ SITUATION Full sun or partial shade
- ☀ SOIL Slightly acid and moisture-retentive
- ☀ HARDINESS -40° to -50°F (-40° to -45°C)
- ☀ ZONES 3–7

## VIBURNUM DAVIDII
*Evergreen shrub*

A rounded and slightly dome-shaped shrub, especially when young, with leathery, narrowly oval, dark green leaves with prominent veins. During early summer it reveals dull white flowers in densely clustered heads up to 3in (7.5cm) wide. These are followed by oval, turquoise-blue, ¼in (6mm) long berries, if both male and female plants are present.

No regular pruning is required, other than occasionally cutting out a misplaced or frost-damaged shoot in early spring.

- ☀ HEIGHT 2–3¼ft (60cm–1m)
- ☀ SPREAD 4–5ft (1.2–1.5m)
- ☀ SITUATION Full sun and shelter from cold wind
- ☀ SOIL Moisture-retentive
- ☀ HARDINESS 10° to 0°F (-12° to -17°C)
- ☀ ZONES 8–9

## EUPHORBIA CHARACIAS WULFENII
EUPHORBIA WULFENII
*Evergreen perennial*

An attractive bushy, statuesque, evergreen, woody-based perennial that forms a large clump of upright stems bearing tiered, narrow, blue-gray leaves. From spring to midsummer it bears large, terminal heads, about 9in (23cm) long, of bright yellow-green bracts.

It is a dramatic plant and one that looks good when positioned at the base or top of a flight of steps.

- ☀ HEIGHT 4ft (1.2m)
- ☀ SPREAD 4–5ft (1.2–1.5m)
- ☀ SITUATION Full sun and a warm, wind-sheltered position
- ☀ SOIL Well-drained
- ☀ HARDINESS 10° to 0°F (-12° to -17°C)
- ☀ ZONES 5–9

## FESTUCA GLAUCA
BLUE FESCUE
*Perennial grass*

A perennial ornamental grass that forms a tufted plant packed with upright, narrow, bristlelike, blue-green leaves. During mid- and late summer it develops tall clusters of oval, purple spikelets.

There are several varieties of this grass, including 'Blue-glow' (also known as 'Blauglut') with blue-green leaves.

- ☀ HEIGHT 6–9in (15–23cm)
- ☀ SPREAD 6–8in (15–20cm)
- ☀ SITUATION Full sun
- ☀ SOIL Well-drained and light
- ☀ HARDINESS -10° to -20°F (-23° to -28°C)
- ☀ ZONES 4–9

## HOSTA SIEBOLDIANA ELEGANS
### HOSTA GLAUCA 'ELEGANS'
SIEBOLD PLANTAIN-LILY
*Herbaceous perennial*

A well-known ground-smothering border plant with large, broad, and nearly oval to heart-shaped, glaucous gray-blue leaves. During mid- and late summer it develops pale-lilac flowers.

As well as being planted in a border, it can be put into a large tub on a patio, where it creates a dominant feature.

☼ HEIGHT 1½–2ft (45–60cm)

☼ SPREAD 1½–2ft (45–60cm)

☼ SITUATION Full sun or partial shade

☼ SOIL Fertile, and moisture-retentive but well-drained

☼ HARDINESS 20° to 10°F (-6° to -12°C)

☼ ZONES 3–9

## OXALIS ADENOPHYLLA
*Rhizome*

This dainty perennial has a bulb-like rhizome, which each year produces attractive rosettes of grayish-green, deeply lobed leaves. In fall these die down, and fresh leaves appear in the spring.

From late spring through to early summer it produces 1in (2.5cm) wide, cup-shaped, satin-pink flowers on long stems.

It is an ideal plant for planting in rock gardens, tubs, sink gardens, and raised beds.

☼ HEIGHT 3in (7.5cm)

☼ SPREAD 6in (15cm)

☼ SITUATION Full sun or partial shade

☼ SOIL Well-drained

☼ HARDINESS -10° to -20°F (-23° to -28°C)

☼ ZONES 6–10

### HEBE PIMELEOIDES
*Evergreen shrub*

A low-growing, densely branched shrub with small, oval to pear-shaped, glaucous-blue leaves. From early to late summer it bears purplish-blue flowers in 1in (2.5cm) long spikes.

There are several superb forms, including 'Glaucocaerulea', which is prostrate and with glaucous-blue leaves and lavender-blue flowers.

No regular pruning is needed, other than cutting out winter-damaged shoots in spring. Cut off dead flowers as soon as they fade.

- ❋ HEIGHT 1–1½ft (30–45cm)
- ❋ SPREAD 2–2½ft (60–75cm)
- ❋ SITUATION Full sun
- ❋ SOIL Well-drained
- ❋ HARDINESS 10° to 0°F
  (-12° to -17°C)
- ❋ ZONES 8–10

### MELIANTHUS MAJOR
LARGE HONEY-BUSH
*Evergreen subshrub*

A slightly tender, sparsely branched, spreading shrub with large, deeply serrated, glaucous-blue leaves, which are up to 1½ft (45cm) long and formed of several leaflets. These are borne on sea-green and glaucous hollow stems.

During summer it develops tubular, tawny-crimson flowers in dense, erect clusters up to 6in (15cm) long.

- ❋ HEIGHT 5–7ft (1.5–2.1m)
- ❋ SPREAD 7–9ft (2.1–2.7m)
- ❋ SITUATION Full sun, with shelter from cold wind; it requires a mild area
- ❋ SOIL Fertile, and moisture-retentive but well-drained
- ❋ HARDINESS 30° to 20°F
  (-1° to -6°C)
- ❋ ZONES 8–11

## RUTA GRAVEOLENS
RUE
*Evergreen subshrub*

A popular hardy shrub with half-woody stems and deeply divided, blue-green leaves that have an acrid odor when cut or bruised. During early and midsummer it develops clusters of dull-yellow flowers.

The form 'Jackman's Blue' has a compact nature and bright blue-gray leaves.

No regular pruning is needed, other than cutting back to shape in spring.

❄ HEIGHT 2–2½ft (60–75cm)

❄ SPREAD 1½–2½ft (45–75cm)

❄ SITUATION Full sun

❄ SOIL Well-drained

❄ HARDINESS -10° to -20°F (-23° to -28°C)

❄ ZONES 4–9

## YUCCA WHIPPLEI
OUR LORD'S CANDLE
*Evergreen shrub*

This tender, often stemless shrub usually forms a dense, rounded clump of narrow, rigid, 1–3ft (30–90cm) long, spine-tipped, and finely toothed glaucous leaves. During early summer it develops long, stiff stems that bear large, greenish-white, and fragrant flowers edged with purple.

❄ HEIGHT 4–6ft (1.2–1.8m)

❄ SPREAD 3–4ft (90cm–1.2m)

❄ SITUATION Full sun and shelter from cold wind; it is only suitable for mild areas

❄ SOIL Well-drained; wet, cold soil is more dangerous to plants than slight frost

❄ HARDINESS 20° to 10°F (-6° to -12°C)

❄ ZONES 4–10

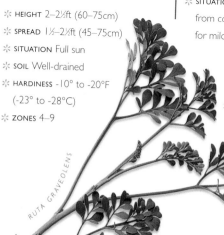

RUTA GRAVEOLENS

*Different shades of blue make a lovely planting combination.*

# index for blue

*See the following pages for other plants with several varieties, including blue:*

LOBELIA 'CAMBRIDGE BLUE'

# WHITE

*White lightens up any space in which it is found: think of the first snowdrops in a wintery garden.*

# the color white
# white plants

Carpentaria californica *represents a wonderful example of pure white flowers. There are also many off-white colors to be found among flowers.*

White is not included as a color by purists—white being considered pure light, or the absence of color. But in garden terms it is much easier to include white as a color, as so many plants have white flowers, and many have leaves that are variegated green-and-white.

When looking at white flowers, foliage, or fruit it is important to be able to distinguish between pure white (as seen in the flowers of *Impatiens* 'Accent White' and *Lysimachia clethroides*, for example) and "off-white" flowers (as seen in many of the hellebores and nicotianas), which are pale tints of other colors. Pure white glows and shines, whereas off-white generally blends more easily with other colors.

Green-and-white variegated leaves can include either pure white, as epitomized by the foliage of *Hedera helix* 'Glacier' and the silvery white of *Lamium maculatum* 'Beacon Silver', or cream, as seen in *Brunnera macrophylla* 'Hadspen Cream'.

### COLOR HARMONIES

As white is not officially a color, it blends with all other colors of the spectrum except, we would suggest, yellow. Yellow adds the light of the sun, whereas white is pure light, so together they fight one another—each dimming the beauty of the other.

*These white flowers, set among dense foliage, give added interest to the bed in which they are planted.*

## USING WHITE IN YOUR GARDEN

Large areas of white—a planting of white peonies, for instance—draw the eye and are best used in the center of a bed or border to bring it into focus; dots and splashes of white, such as the flowers of gypsophila or the white forget-me-not, lift a blue or purple border and increase its interest. Green-and-white variegated foliage is particularly useful as it adds year-round lightness to any planting, but avoid mixing yellow-and-green variegated foliage with the green-and-white.

## GRAY FOLIAGE

*SENECIO CINERERIA*

Gray, like white, is a not a color but a mixture of black and white. The gray we find in the garden is usually caused by white hairs on the surface of leaves, and most of these plants need well-drained, sunny conditions. Avoid mixing gray foliage and white flowers or green-and-white foliage, as the gray makes the white look dirty, while the white makes the gray foliage dull.

195

## BEGONIA × SEMPERFLORENS
### 'OLYMPIA WHITE'
WAX BEGONIA
*Semihardy annual*

This tender perennial is usually grown as a semihardy annual to create a wealth of flowers in summer-flowering bedding schemes. Throughout summer it produces a mass of white flowers.

There are many other varieties, in colors including red, scarlet, and pink. Some are further enhanced by attractively colored bronze foliage, or by green leaves tinged with red.

- ※ HEIGHT 6–9in (15–23cm)
- ※ SPREAD 6–9in (15–23cm)
- ※ SITUATION Dappled sunlight
- ※ SOIL Light, and well-drained but moisture-retentive
- ※ HARDINESS Will not tolerate temperatures below 32°F (0°C)
- ※ ZONES Spring to fall annual in zones 2–8; short-lived perennial in zones 9–11

## DIANTHUS
### 'PRINCESS WHITE'
ANNUAL PINK
*Annual*

A beautiful hybrid annual pink derived, in part, from *Dianthus chinensis*, a short-lived perennial or biennial. Plants develop loose clusters of clear white flowers from early summer to the frosts of fall. These are borne amid narrow, mid-green leaves.

Plants have a dwarf and compact nature and are ideal for edging borders and also for growing in rock gardens.

- ※ HEIGHT 8–10in (20–25cm)
- ※ SPREAD 10–12in (25–30cm)
- ※ SITUATION Full sun
- ※ SOIL Well-drained, and neutral or slightly alkaline
- ※ HARDINESS Tolerates slight frost
- ※ ZONES Hardy, cool-season annual in zones 2–11

**IMPATIENS
'ACCENT WHITE'**
*Semihardy annual*

This greenhouse perennial is often raised as a semihardy annual to make a splash of color. This variety produces five-petalled and flat-faced white flowers, each up to 1½in (36mm) across.

Varieties include red, purple, orange, and pink.

☀ **HEIGHT** 6–10in (15–25cm)

☀ **SPREAD** 9–12in (23–30cm)

☀ **SITUATION** Full sun or partial shade

☀ **SOIL** Fertile and well-drained

☀ **HARDINESS** Will not tolerate temperatures below 32°F (0°C)

☀ **ZONES** Tender perennial, grown as warm-season semihardy annual in zones 2–11

**LOBULARIA MARITIMA
'SNOW CARPET'**
**ALYSSUM MARITIMUM
'SNOW CARPET'**
SWEET ALYSSUM
*Semihardy annual*

This low-growing and bushy hardy annual is invariably grown as a semihardy annual for planting into borders in order to create a canvas of white flowers throughout summer and until the frosts of fall.

Other varieties have lilac, rose, or purple heads.

☀ **HEIGHT** 3–6in (7.5–15cm)

☀ **SPREAD** 8–12in (20–30cm)

☀ **SITUATION** Full sun

☀ **SOIL** Moderately fertile and well-drained

☀ **HARDINESS** Will not tolerate temperatures below 32°F (0°C)

☀ **ZONES** Semihardy cool-season annual in zones 2–9; perennial in zones 10–11

*IMPATIENS 'ACCENT WHITE'*

**annuals**

## MATRICARIA
### 'WHITE STARS'
MATRICARIA EXIMIA
'WHITE STARS'
FEVERFEW
*Annual*

A hardy but short-lived perennial invariably raised as an annual. It has changed its name several times and, in addition to the above botanical names, you might find it listed as *Chrysanthemum parthenium*.

This variety creates a wealth of white, cushionlike flowers, each about ⅜in (18mm) wide. They are borne above light green, pungently aromatic, chrysanthemum-like leaves.

There are several other varieties, mainly white but also yellow.

❀ HEIGHT 8–10in (20–25cm)

❀ SPREAD 8–12in (20–30cm)

❀ SITUATION Full sun

❀ SOIL Well-drained but moisture-retentive

❀ HARDINESS Tolerates slight frost

❀ ZONES Tender perennial, grown as a warm-season annual in zones 2–11

## NICOTIANA
### 'DOMINO WHITE'
NICOTIANA × SANDERAE
'DOMINO WHITE'
TOBACCO
*Semihardy annual*

This semihardy annual is popular in summer-flowering bedding displays, as well as in containers on patios. Its sweetly fragrant, open-faced, white flowers create a restful and cool ambience, as well as a good contrast to flowers with stronger colors.

The range of other colors is wide and, within the domino series, colors include scarlet, rose, pink, and lime, as well as bicolored flowers.

❀ HEIGHT 10–12in (25–30cm)

❀ SPREAD 10–15in (25–38cm)

❀ SITUATION Full sun, warm and shelter from wind

❀ SOIL Fertile and well-drained

❀ HARDINESS Will not tolerate temperatures below 32°F (0°C)

❀ ZONES Warm-season annual in zones 2–9; perennial in zones 10–11

## ANEMONE BLANDA
### 'WHITE SPLENDOR'
GREEK ANEMONE
*Tuber*

With a rather rounded tuber, this diminutive anemone has fernlike, lobed, and deeply divided green leaves. This variety reveals large, white flowers, about 1⅝in (42mm) wide, during early and mid-spring. In some areas it flowers during the late winter.

There are several other varieties, extending the color range to pale blue, mauve, and pink. Additionally, there are further white-flowered forms of this anemone.

✳ HEIGHT 6–8in (15–20cm)

✳ SPREAD Space the tubers 4in (10cm) apart

✳ SITUATION Light or partial shade

✳ SOIL Fertile, and well-drained but moisture-retentive

✳ HARDINESS -10° to -20°F (-23° to -28°C)

✳ ZONES 4–8

## CROCUS CHRYSANTHUS
### 'SNOW BUNTING'
*Corm*

A popular early spring-flowering, cormous plant with short, narrow, grayish-green leaves and globular white flowers with deep purple outsides and an orange base.

The range of varieties is wide and includes colors such as golden-yellow, mauve-blue, purple-blue, and dark bronze.

Plant the crocus corms 2–3in (5–7.5cm) deep.

✳ HEIGHT 3in (7.5cm)

✳ SPREAD Space the corms 3in (7.5cm) apart

✳ SITUATION Full sun or dappled light

✳ SOIL Well-drained but moisture-retentive

✳ HARDINESS -20° to -30°F (-28° to -34°C)

✳ ZONES 3–11; best in zones 3–7

## GALANTHUS NIVALIS 'FLORE PLENO'
### GALANTHUS NIVALIS 'PLENUS'
COMMON SNOWDROP
*Bulb*

This superb double-flowered form of the common snowdrop reveals petal-packed white flowers. However, to some eyes it has a less elegant form than the common type. Nevertheless, it is a dramatic and dominant snowdrop, with flowers during late winter.

The height of this plant varies; in rich, moist soil and in shade it is at its tallest.

- ☼ HEIGHT 3–8in (7.5–20cm)
- ☼ SPREAD Space the bulbs 3–5in (7.5–13cm) apart
- ☼ SITUATION Dappled light
- ☼ SOIL Moderately heavy and moisture-retentive
- ☼ HARDINESS -20° to -30°F (-28° to -34°C)
- ☼ ZONES 3–8

## IRIS 'WHITE WEDGWOOD'
DUTCH IRIS
*Bulb*

This bulbous, hybrid Dutch iris is derived from *Iris xiphium* (Spanish iris) and *I. tingitana*. It is one of the earliest hybrids to flower and during early summer reveals white flowers up to 5in (13cm) across.

There are several other hybrid Dutch irises, in colors including blue, purple, and yellow, as well as white.

Plant the bulbs 4–6in (10–15cm) deep in early fall.

- ☼ HEIGHT 1¼–2ft (38–60cm)
- ☼ SPREAD Space the bulbs 4–6in (10–15cm) apart
- ☼ SITUATION Full sun
- ☼ SOIL Light, fertile, and well-drained
- ☼ HARDINESS 20° to 10°F (-6° to -12°C)
- ☼ ZONES 7–11; mulch in zone 6

**LILIUM REGALE**
REGAL LILY
*Bulb*

A well-known and popular stem-rooting lily with upright stems bearing loose clusters of fragrant, funnel-shaped, white flowers, each up to 5in (13cm) long, during mid-summer. The backs of the petals are lightly shaded rose-purple, while their centers are a dull yellow.

Plant the bulbs 6–9in (15–23cm) deep from mid-fall through to early spring.

❋ **HEIGHT** 5–6ft (1.5–1.8m)
❋ **SPREAD** Space the bulbs 1ft (30cm) apart
❋ **SITUATION** Full sun or partial shade; shelter from strong wind
❋ **SOIL** Well-drained but moisture-retentive
❋ **HARDINESS** -10° to -20°F (-23° to -28°C)
❋ **ZONES** 4–8

**NARCISSUS 'MOUNT HOOD'**
TRUMPET DAFFODIL
*Bulb*

A familiar and widely planted daffodil that produces large, rounded, creamy-white flowers during late winter and early spring.

It is ideal for planting in large drifts, under deciduous trees or in the open, in order to create a flood of color.

Plant the bulbs in late summer or early fall, setting each bulb three times its own depth deep.

❋ **HEIGHT** 1¼–1½ft (38–45cm)
❋ **SPREAD** Space bulbs 3–4in (7.5–10cm) apart
❋ **SITUATION** Full sun or light shade
❋ **SOIL** Fertile, and well-drained but moisture-retentive
❋ **HARDINESS** -20° to -30°F (-28° to -34°C)
❋ **ZONES** 3–9

## ANEMONE × HYBRIDA 'HONORINE JOBERT'
**ANEMONE JAPONICA 'HONORINE JOBERT'**
JAPANESE ANEMONE
*Herbaceous perennial*

A popular clump-forming and erect border plant, with broad, vinelike, dark green leaves. From late summer to mid-fall it bears saucer-shaped white flowers, each 2–3in (5–7.5cm) wide.

Other varieties extend the color range to subtle tones of pink and rose, as well as mauve and cream. There are both single- and double-flowered forms.

- ☀ HEIGHT 4ft (1.2m)
- ☀ SPREAD 1–1½ft (30–45cm)
- ☀ SITUATION Partial shade
- ☀ SOIL Fertile, and well-drained but moisture-retentive; it tolerates lime
- ☀ HARDINESS 0° to -10°F (-17° to -23°C)
- ☀ ZONES 4–8

## ANTHEMIS PUNCTATA CUPANIANA
**ANTHEMIS CUPANIANA**
GOLDEN MARGUERITE
*Herbaceous perennial*

A spreading and cushion-forming, short-lived perennial for planting in borders as well as in containers on patios, where it creates a superb display. From early to late summer it reveals bright-faced, daisylike white flowers, up to 2in (5cm) wide and with bright yellow centers. These appear above slightly aromatic, finely dissected, gray leaves.

- ☀ HEIGHT 5–10in (13–25cm)
- ☀ SPREAD 1–1½ft (30–45cm)
- ☀ SITUATION Full sun and shelter from cold wind
- ☀ SOIL Well-drained
- ☀ HARDINESS 10° to 0°F (-12° to -17°C)
- ☀ ZONES 6–10

## ASTILBE × ARENDSII 'IRRLICHT'
HYBRID ASTILBE
*Herbaceous perennial*

A clump-forming border plant with deep-green, fernlike leaves and clouds of featherlike white flowers borne in pyramidal heads between early and late summer.

There are many superb varieties, in colors including clear pink, dark red, and rose-red. Additionally, they range in height, from those at 1¼ft (38cm) high to others 4ft (1.2m) tall.

- ☀ HEIGHT 1⅓ft (40cm)
- ☀ SPREAD 1¼–1½ft (38–45cm)
- ☀ SITUATION Full sun or light shade
- ☀ SOIL Fertile and moisture-retentive
- ☀ HARDINESS 0° to -10°F (-17° to -23°C)
- ☀ ZONES 4–8

## CIMICIFUGA SIMPLEX 'WHITE PEARL'
KAMCHATKA BUGBANE
*Herbaceous perennial*

A distinctive, tall, upright, and graceful border plant with somewhat fernlike, mid-green leaves. During fall, and sometimes even into early winter, it bears arching stems that reveal fragrant, nodding, and fluffy heads of pure white flowers.

It is one of the best late-flowering border plants and a joy to behold when the flowers are caught by low rays of the sun.

- ☀ HEIGHT 4ft (1.2m)
- ☀ SPREAD 2ft (60cm)
- ☀ SITUATION Full sun or light shade
- ☀ SOIL Fertile and moisture-retentive
- ☀ HARDINESS -10° to -20°F (-23° to -28°C)
- ☀ ZONES 3–8

### DICENTRA SPECTABILIS 'ALBA'
COMMON BLEEDING-HEART
*Herbaceous perennial*

A dainty and graceful border plant, with large, fernlike, gray-green leaves that create an attractive foil for the ivory-white, heart-shaped, and locketlike flowers. These are borne along the tops of tall, divided stems, from late spring to midsummer.

The ordinary species has rose-red flowers with protruding and glistening-white inner petals.

❊ HEIGHT 1½–2½ft (45–75cm)

❊ SPREAD 1½ft (45cm)

❊ SITUATION Full sun or partial shade, and shelter from cold wind in spring

❊ SOIL Fertile, and well-drained but moisture-retentive

❊ HARDINESS 0° to -10°F (-17° to -23°C)

❊ ZONES 2–9

### DICTAMNUS ALBUS
GASPLANT
*Herbaceous perennial*

A long-lived, handsome, and distinctive border plant with glossy, dark green leaves. During early and midsummer it develops upright stems that bear fragrant, spiderlike, white flowers.

The old flowers are rich in a volatile oil that, during warm, still evenings, can be ignited.

The variety 'Purpureus', earlier known as *Dictamnus fraxinella*, has pink flowers striped red.

❊ HEIGHT 2ft (60cm)

❊ SPREAD 1½ft (45cm)

❊ SITUATION Full sun

❊ SOIL Well-drained and slightly chalky

❊ HARDINESS -30° to -40°F (-34° to -40°C)

❊ ZONES 3–8

## HELLEBORUS NIGER
CHRISTMAS-ROSE
*Evergreen perennial*

This distinctive border plant, which is ideal for planting in a winter-flowering border, has leathery, dark green evergreen leaves formed of seven to nine lobes. From midwinter through to early spring it bears white, saucer-shaped flowers at the tops of stiff stems. Each flower is up to 2in (5cm) wide, with golden anthers.

- ❋ **HEIGHT** 1–1½ft (30–45cm)
- ❋ **SPREAD** 1½ft (45cm)
- ❋ **SITUATION** Light shade
- ❋ **SOIL** Well-drained but moisture-retentive
- ❋ **HARDINESS** -30° to -40°F (-34° to -40°C)
- ❋ **ZONES** 3–8

## LEUCANTHEMUM × SUPERBUM 'ESTHER READ'
CHRYSANTHEMUM MAXIMUM 'ESTHER READ'
SHASTA DAISY
*Herbaceous perennial*

A traditional and popular, clump-forming border plant with tall stems bearing dark green and toothed leaves. From early to late summer it develops double white flowers, up to 3in (7.5cm) wide, with golden eyes.

There are several varieties, most bearing white flowers; some have single-flowers, others double-flowers, while a few even have frilled petals.

- ❋ **HEIGHT** 2½ft (75cm)
- ❋ **SPREAD** 1¼–1½ft (38–45cm)
- ❋ **SITUATION** Full sun
- ❋ **SOIL** Fertile, and moisture-retentive but well-drained
- ❋ **HARDINESS** -10° to -20°F (-23° to -28°C)
- ❋ **ZONES** 4–9

## LYSIMACHIA CLETHROIDES
JAPANESE LOOSESTRIFE
*Herbaceous perennial*

A clump-forming border plant with mid-green, lance-shaped leaves, which usually assume red and orange tints in fall. From midsummer to early fall it reveals distinctive, 4–6in (10–15cm) long, arching heads of white, star-shaped flowers.

- ☼ HEIGHT 2½–3ft (75–90cm)
- ☼ SPREAD 1½ft (45cm)
- ☼ SITUATION Full sun or partial shade
- ☼ SOIL Moisture-retentive but well-drained
- ☼ HARDINESS -20° to -30°F (-28° to -34°C)
- ☼ ZONES 3–8

## OSTEOSPERMUM 'WHIRLYGIG'
ANNUAL OSTEOSPERMUM
*Tender perennial*

This tender perennial is grown as a semihardy annual and raised for planting into summer-flowering displays. This particular variety produces large, distinctive, daisylike flowers with quilled, spoon-shaped petals, which have a white face and a blue reverse.

The flowers tend to close in dull weather and appear from the latter part of early summer through to early fall. The range of related, seed-raised varieties is wide, in colors including white, yellow, pink, orange, blue, and purple.

- ☼ HEIGHT 1–1½ft (30–45cm)
- ☼ SPREAD 10in (25cm)
- ☼ SITUATION Full sun and shelter from strong, blustery wind
- ☼ SOIL Well-drained
- ☼ HARDINESS Will not tolerate temperatures below 32°F (0°C)
- ☼ ZONES 8–10

OSTEOSPERMUM 'WHIRLYGIG'

## CARPENTERIA CALIFORNICA
### EVERGREEN MOCK-ORANGE
*Evergreen shrub*

This slightly tender, bushy shrub with lance-shaped, glossy-green leaves develops masses of glistening-white, anemonelike flowers up to 3in (7.5cm) wide during early and mid-summer.

No regular pruning is needed, other than cutting back straggly and frost-damaged shoots immediately the flowers fade.

❋ HEIGHT 6–10ft (1.8–3m)

❋ SPREAD 6–8ft (1.8–2.4m)

❋ SITUATION Full sun, and shelter from cold wind, especially in spring; preferably plant in the shelter of a warm, sunny wall

❋ SOIL Well drained; it is tolerant of lime

❋ HARDINESS 20° to 10°F (-6° to -12°C)

❋ ZONES 8–10

## EXOCHORDA × MACRANTHA 'THE BRIDE'
### PEARL BUSH
*Deciduous shrub*

A rounded and bushy shrub, with a lax and open nature, and narrowly pear-shaped, glabrous, mid-green leaves. During late spring and early summer it reveals 3–4in (7.5–10cm) long clusters of six to ten snowy white flowers, each about 1¼in (30mm) wide.

No regular pruning is needed, other than occasionally cutting out old or damaged shoots when the flowers fade.

❋ HEIGHT 6–10ft (1.8–3m)

❋ SPREAD 6–8ft (1.8–2.4m)

❋ SITUATION Full sun and shelter from cold, spring wind

❋ SOIL Well-drained; it dislikes shallow, chalky soil

❋ HARDINESS -10° to -20°F (-23° to -28°C)

❋ ZONES 4–8

## HYDRANGEA PANICULATA 'GRANDIFLORA'
PANICLE HYDRANGEA
*Deciduous shrub*

A large and spectacular shrub, with arching stems bearing mid-green leaves and large, pyramidal heads, up to 18in (45cm) long, packed with white flowers. These appear during late summer and into early fall.

This shrub needs regular pruning; in late winter or early spring, cut back by half those shoots that flowered during the previous year. If exceptionally large flower heads are desired, then thin out the flowering shoots.

- ❋ **HEIGHT** 8–10ft (2.4–3m)
- ❋ **SPREAD** 8–10ft (2.4–3m)
- ❋ **SITUATION** Full sun or light shade
- ❋ **SOIL** Fertile, and moisture-retentive but well-drained
- ❋ **HARDINESS** -30° to -40°F (-34° to -40°C)
- ❋ **ZONES** 3–8

## MAGNOLIA STELLATA
MAGNOLIA KOBUS STELLATA
STAR MAGNOLIA
*Deciduous shrub*

A slow-growing, rounded, and compact shrub with lance-shaped, mid-green leaves up to 4in (10cm) long. During early and mid-spring it bears fragrant, white, star-shaped flowers up to 4in (10cm) wide. It is an ideal magnolia for planting in a small garden.

There is also a pink-flowered form of this shrub.

No regular pruning is needed.

- ❋ **HEIGHT** 8–10ft (2.4–3m)
- ❋ **SPREAD** 8–10ft (2.4–3m)
- ❋ **SITUATION** Full sun and shelter from cold wind, especially during spring
- ❋ **SOIL** Well-drained but moisture-retentive
- ❋ **HARDINESS** -20° to -30°F (-28° to -34°C)
- ❋ **ZONES** 4–8

## PHILADELPHUS 'MINNESOTA SNOWFLAKE'
**PHILADELPHUS × VIRGINALIS 'MINNESOTA SNOWFLAKE'**
MOCK-ORANGE
*Deciduous shrub*

A beautiful hybrid shrub with a mounded nature, occasionally growing 6ft (1.8m) or more high—but usually less. During early and midsummer it develops clusters of up to nine fragrant, fully double, white flowers on arching branches.

Regular pruning is essential; after the flowers fade, cut out a few old shoots to encourage the development of young growths, which will bear flowers during the following year.

- ☀ **HEIGHT** 3–5ft (90cm–1.5m)
- ☀ **SPREAD** 3¼–5ft (1–1.5m)
- ☀ **SITUATION** Full sun or partial shade
- ☀ **SOIL** Well-drained
- ☀ **HARDINESS** -10° to -20°F (-23° to -28°C)
- ☀ **ZONES** 4–8

## PIERIS JAPONICA
**ANDROMEDA JAPONICA**
JAPANESE ANDROMEDA
*Evergreen shrub*

A bushy and well-clothed shrub with leathery, narrowly oval or slightly pear-shaped, dark green, and glossy leaves. They are coppery red when young.

During mid- and late spring this shrub develops terminal clusters of drooping, lily-of-the-valley-like white flowers.

No regular pruning is needed, other than cutting out straggly shoots when the flowers fade.

- ☀ **HEIGHT** 6–10ft (1.8–3m)
- ☀ **SPREAD** 6–10ft (1.8–3m)
- ☀ **SITUATION** Partial shade and shelter from cold wind, especially in spring
- ☀ **SOIL** Slightly acid and moisture-retentive
- ☀ **HARDINESS** 0° to -10°F (-17° to -23°C)
- ☀ **ZONES** 5–8

### SPIRAEA × VANHOUTTEI
VANHOUTTE SPIRAEA
*Deciduous shrub*

A graceful and arching shrub with distinctly lobed, dark green leaves. During early summer it develops dense, 2in (5cm) wide clusters of white flowers, each about ½in (12mm) across.

Regular pruning is essential. After the flowers fade, thin out some of the older wood to allow light and air to enter the shrub.

- ☀ HEIGHT 5–6ft (1.5–1.8m)
- ☀ SPREAD 6–7ft (1.8–2.1m)
- ☀ SITUATION Sunny and open
- ☀ SOIL Fertile, and moisture-retentive but well-drained
- ☀ HARDINESS -20° to -30°F (-28° to -34°C)
- ☀ ZONES 3–8

### VIBURNUM × CARLCEPHALUM
*Deciduous shrub*

A popular deciduous hybrid shrub with broadly oval, light green leaves. During mid- and late spring it bears a mass of fragrant, creamy white flowers borne in 3–4in (7.5–10cm) wide clusters.

No regular pruning is needed, other than removing dead wood and thinning out congested shrubs as soon as the flowers have faded.

- ☀ HEIGHT 6–8ft (1.8–2.4m)
- ☀ SPREAD 6–7ft (1.8–2.1m)
- ☀ SITUATION Full sun and shelter from cold wind, especially in early spring
- ☀ SOIL Moisture-retentive but well-drained
- ☀ HARDINESS -10° to -20°F (-23° to -28°C)
- ☀ ZONES 6–8

**JASMINUM OFFICINALE**
COMMON WHITE JASMINE
*Deciduous climber*

A well-known and widely grown sprawling and twining climber with mid-green leaves formed of five, seven, or nine, mid-green leaflets. From early summer to fall it bears clusters of scented, pure-white flowers borne in 2–3in (5–7.5cm) long clusters.

It needs the benefit of a trellis or pergola up which to climb.

After the flowers fade, thin out the shoots on congested plants.

☀ HEIGHT 20–25ft (6–7.5m)

☀ SPREAD 15–20ft (4.5–6m)

☀ SITUATION Full sun and shelter from cold wind

☀ SOIL Well-drained

☀ HARDINESS 10° to 0°F (-12° to -17°C)

☀ ZONES 8–10

**ROSA**
**'MME ALFRED CARRIÈRE'**
CLIMBING ROSE
*Deciduous climber*

A magnificent climber of the Noisette type, but with the characteristics of the more modern climbing roses. It is vigorous and will cover a large wall with light green leaves. During early and midsummer—and often recurrently later in the season—it bears large, sweetly scented, fully double, creamy-blush flowers that fade to nearly white.

☀ HEIGHT 15–18ft (4.5–5.4m)

☀ SPREAD 10ft (3m)

☀ SITUATION Full sun and an open position

☀ SOIL Well-drained but moisture-retentive, especially when planted against a wall

☀ HARDINESS 10° to 0°F (-12° to -17°C)

☀ ZONES 5–9

**ASTRANTIA MAJOR
'SUNNINGDALE VARIEGATED'**
**ASTRANTIA MAJOR 'VARIEGATA'**
MASTERWORT
*Herbaceous perennial*

An attractive border plant with large, oval to lance-shaped, pointed leaves variegated cream and yellow. As the season progresses the variegations tend to disappear. However, cutting back the old flower stems helps the retention of the variegation.

During early and midsummer it develops starlike, white flowers that are flushed pink.

☀ HEIGHT 2–2½ft (60–75cm)

☀ SPREAD 1¼–1½ft (38–45cm)

☀ SITUATION Full sun or partial shade

☀ SOIL Well-drained but moisture-retentive; when in full sun, the plants must have moist soil

☀ HARDINESS 0° to -10°F (-17° to -23°C)

☀ ZONES 4–7

**BRUNNERA MACROPHYLLA
'HADSPEN CREAM'**
HEARTLEAF BRUNNERA
*Herbaceous perennial*

A distinctive bushy and ground-covering, low-temperature-tolerant, border plant with large, heart-shaped, light, mat-green leaves attractively splashed with cream. During late spring and early summer it reveals sprays of blue, forget-me-not-like, flowers.

☀ HEIGHT 1½–1¾ft (45–50cm)

☀ SPREAD 1½ft (45cm)

☀ SITUATION Preferably a position in light shade, although it will grow in full sun if the soil is kept moist throughout the summer

☀ SOIL Well-drained but moisture-retentive

☀ HARDINESS -30° to -40°F (-34° to -40°C)

☀ ZONES 3–8

## FRAGARIA × ANANASSA 'VARIEGATA'
VARIEGATED GARDEN STRAWBERRY
*Semievergreen perennial*

A relatively short-lived border novelty, with a semievergreen nature in all but the harshest winters. The leaves resemble those of the normal garden strawberry plant, but are green variegated with cream.

It also develops the well-known berries, but these are usually not worthy of being eaten.

It is ideal for planting in borders, as well as in containers on a patio.

❄ HEIGHT 6in (15cm)

❄ SPREAD 1–1¼ft (30–38cm)

❄ SITUATION Full sun or partial shade

❄ SOIL Fertile, and moisture-retentive but well-drained

❄ HARDINESS 30° to 20°F (-1° to -6°C)

❄ ZONES 4–8

## LAMIUM MACULATUM 'BEACON SILVER'
SPOTTED DEAD NETTLE
*Herbaceous perennial*

An attractive and fast-growing, ground-covering border plant. It creates a sea of silvery white, small, heart-shaped leaves.

From late spring to early summer it bears pink flowers, but it is the leaves that create the best display.

There is also a golden form, which creates dominant beacons of yellow foliage throughout the summer.

❄ HEIGHT 6–9in (15–23cm)

❄ SPREAD 1–1¼ft (30–38cm)

❄ SITUATION Partial shade

❄ SOIL Fertile, cool, and moisture-retentive

❄ HARDINESS -20° to -30°F (-28° to -34°C)

❄ ZONES 3–8

## ACTINIDIA KOLOMIKTA
KOLOMIKTA ACTINIDIA
*Deciduous climber*

A spreading and attractively variegated climber with dark green, slightly heart-shaped leaves up to 6in (15cm) long. They have white or pink markings at their tips and on their upper parts.

It is not self-supporting and therefore needs a trellis up which to clamber.

No regular pruning is needed, other than thinning out shoots in late winter or early spring.

☀ HEIGHT 8–12ft (2.4–3.6m)

☀ SPREAD 8–12ft (2.4–3.6m)

☀ SITUATION Full sun or partial shade

☀ SOIL Fertile, well-drained, and neutral or slightly acid; avoid shallow and chalky soil

☀ HARDINESS -20° to -30°F (-28° to -34°C)

☀ ZONES 4–8

## EUONYMUS FORTUNEI 'SILVER QUEEN'
EUONYMUS RADICANS 'SILVER QUEEN'
WINTERCREEPER
*Evergreen shrub*

This versatile shrub can be planted in a border, where it has both a compact and slightly spreading nature. Alternatively, it can be planted to create a screen of foliage against a wall, where it grows 5–6ft (1.5–1.8m) high. It is a very attractive shrub, with the unfolding leaves in spring being a rich creamy yellow. Later they become green, with broad creamy white edges.

No regular pruning is needed, other than occasionally cutting out a misplaced shoot in spring.

☀ HEIGHT 1–1½ft (30–45cm)

☀ SPREAD 3–4ft (90cm–1.2m)

☀ SITUATION Full sun or partial shade, and slight shelter from cold wind

☀ SOIL Well-drained

☀ HARDINESS 10° to 0°F (-12° to -17°C)

☀ ZONES 4–8

**HEDERA HELIX
'GLACIER'**
ENGLISH IVY
*Evergreen climber*

This popular, slow-growing, and variegated ivy creates a mass of small, prettily lobed leaves. They are variegated silver-gray and have narrow, white edges. Often this ivy is grown as a houseplant.

When grown in a garden, it initially needs protection from cold wind. It is self-clinging on walls, but can also be used to create ground cover.

There are many other small-leaved, variegated ivies, with leaves revealing medleys of green, yellow, silver, cream, gray, and white.

❋ HEIGHT 10–12ft (3–3.6m) or more
❋ SPREAD 8–10ft (2.4–3m) or more
❋ SITUATION Sunny and warm wall
❋ SOIL Fertile, and well-drained but moisture-retentive, especially when planted at the base of a wall
❋ HARDINESS 0° to -10°F (-17° to -23°C)
❋ ZONES 4–9

**ILEX AQUIFOLIUM
'FEROX ARGENTEA'**
SILVER-EDGE ENGLISH HOLLY
*Evergreen shrub or small tree*

A slow-growing, hardy shrub or small tree with small, dark green leaves with creamy white edges and spines. These are borne on rich purple twigs.

There are several other variegated hollies, one with leaves having gold or yellow central strips.

❋ HEIGHT 8–15ft (2.4–4.5m)
❋ SPREAD 6–8ft (1.8–2.4m)
❋ SITUATION Full sun or light shade
❋ SOIL Moisture-retentive but well-drained
❋ HARDINESS 0° to -10°F (-17° to -23°C)
❋ ZONES 6–9

HEDERA HELIX 'GLACIER'

## ANAPHALIS TRIPLINERVIS
PEARLY EVERLASTING
*Herbaceous perennial*

A bushy but upright border plant with silvery gray leaves; their undersides have an attractive woolly nature. During late summer and into early fall white flowers appear in tightly bunched, domelike heads up to 4in (10cm) wide.

This is an ideal plant for drying and displaying in flower arrangements indoors during the winter.

❄ HEIGHT 1–1¼ft (30–38cm)

❄ SPREAD 1–1¼ft (30–38cm)

❄ SITUATION Full sun; it also grows well in shade if the soil is relatively dry

❄ SOIL Well-drained

❄ HARDINESS -10° to -20°F (-23° to -28°C)

❄ ZONES 3–8

## BALLOTA PSEUDODICTAMNUS
*Deciduous shrub*

This slightly tender, low-growing, and shrubby border plant has a much-branched and spreading nature. The heart-shaped, woolly green leaves are borne on sprawling shoots. During midsummer it bears whorls of lilac-pink flowers, although these are rather insignificant when compared with the foliage.

To encourage the development of attractive stems and leaves, cut all shoots back by half each spring.

❄ HEIGHT 1½–2ft (45–60cm)

❄ SPREAD 2ft (60cm)

❄ SITUATION Full sun

❄ SOIL Well-drained; wet soil, especially during cold winters, will kill the plant

❄ HARDINESS 20° to 10°F (-6° to -12°C)

❄ ZONES 8–10; as an annual in zones 4–7

**ELAEAGNUS COMMUTATA**
SILVERBERRY
*Deciduous shrub*

A slow-growing, extemely hardy, wide-spreading, and suckering shrub with upright, rather slender, reddish-brown stems that bear narrowly oval, silvery-green, scaly leaves.

During late spring it bears a profusion of fragrant, silvery flowers, yellow on the inside, which are followed by edible, silvery, egg-shaped fruits.

No regular pruning is needed, other than cutting out straggly shoots in mid-summer.

☀ HEIGHT 6–8ft (1.8–2.4m)

☀ SPREAD 6–8ft (1.8–2.4m)

☀ SITUATION Full sun

☀ SOIL Ordinary soil; it grows well in poor soil

☀ HARDINESS -40° to -50°F (-40° to -45°C)

☀ ZONES 2–6

**LAVANDULA ANGUSTIFOLIA**
**LAVANDULA OFFICINALIS**
TRUE LAVENDER
*Evergreen shrub*

A popular and widely grown shrub with aromatic, narrow, silver-gray leaves clustered around woody stems. From midsummer to early fall it reveals pale gray-blue flowers in upright, spikelike clusters about 2⅓in (6cm) long.

Old, straggly plants can be pruned severely in late spring to encourage the development of young shoots from the plant's base. Additionally, cut off dead flower stems as soon as the flowers fade.

☀ HEIGHT 3–4ft (90cm–1.2m)

☀ SPREAD 3–4ft (90cm–1.2m)

☀ SITUATION Full sun

☀ SOIL Well-drained

☀ HARDINESS -10° to -20°F (-23° to -28°C)

☀ ZONES 5–9

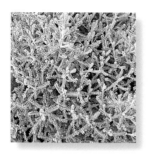

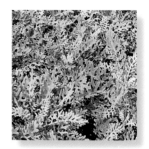

**SANTOLINA
CHAMAECYPARISSUS**
**SANTOLINA INCANA**
LAVENDER-COTTON
*Evergreen shrub*

**SENECIO CINERARIA**
CINERARIA MARITIMA/
**SENECIO BICOLOR**
SILVER GROUNDSEL
*Evergreen subshrub*

| | |
|---|---|
| A mound-forming and densely foliaged shrub with woolly, silvery, threadlike leaves borne on white felted stems. During midsummer it develops bright yellow, buttonlike, solitary flowers, up to ¾in (18mm) wide, at the ends of erect, slender stems about 6in (15cm) long. | A tender shrub, but in temperate regions it is usually treated as a semihardy and short-lived perennial. It is invariably raised as a semihardy annual for planting in summer-flowering bedding displays. Its lobed leaves and stems are covered with white, woolly hairs that give a silvery appearance. |
| No regular pruning is needed. However, when a plant becomes old and straggly, cut stems back into the old wood immediately after the flowers fade. | Yellow flowers appear from mid- to late summer; they are best removed. |
| | Some varieties have deeply divided and fernlike leaves. |

❋ HEIGHT 1½–2ft (45–60cm)

❋ SPREAD 1½–2ft (45–60cm)

❋ SITUATION Full sun

❋ SOIL Well-drained

❋ HARDINESS 10° to 0°F
   (-12° to -17°C)

❋ ZONES 6–8

❋ HEIGHT 1½–2ft (45–60cm)

❋ SPREAD 1¼–1½ft (38–45cm)

❋ SITUATION Full sun, although light
   shade is tolerated

❋ SOIL Well-drained

❋ HARDINESS 20° to 10°F (-6° to -12°C)

❋ ZONES Semihardy annual in zones
   2–4; perennial in zones 5–11, but
   treat as an annual

# index for white

*See the following pages for other plants with several varieties, including white:*

# glossary

ANNUAL  A plant that grows from seed, then flowers and dies within the same year. Some plants that are not strictly annuals (e.g. *Lobelia erinus)* are treated as such.

BIENNIAL  A plant raised from seed that makes its initial growth one year and flowers during the next one, then dies. However, many plants not strictly biennial are treated as such (e.g. *Bellis perennis*).

CALYX  The outer and protective part of a flower. It is usually green and very apparent in roses.

CORM  An underground storage organ formed of a swollen stem base. A gladiolus is an example.

CULTIVAR  A shortened term for "cultivated variety," indicating a variety raised in cultivation. Strictly speaking, most modern varieties are cultivars, but "variety" is still frequently used because it is a term familiar to gardeners.

FLORIFEROUS  Flowering freely, bearing an abundance of flowers.

GENUS (pl. GENERA)  A category of plants in the botanical classification that consists of closely related species.

GLABROUS  Refers to leaves that have a shiny surface.

GLAUCOUS  Meaning grayish-blue, referring to leaves or stems with a powdery greenish or bluish bloom.

HERBACEOUS  A non-woody plant, many of which (but not all) die down to soil level after the completion of each season's growth.

HYBRID  The progeny from parents of different species or genera. It is indicated by a multiplication sign.

HYBRID TEA ROSE  A rose classification, sometimes known as a "Large-flowered Bush" rose.

PERENNIAL  Generally used to refer to herbaceous plants, but also to any plant that lives for several years, including trees, shrubs, and perennial climbers.

PICOTEE  Having outer edges of petals in another color.

RHIZOMATOUS  An underground or partly buried horizontal stem; it can be slender or fleshy. It acts as a storage organ and perpetuates plants from one season to another.

ROOTSTOCK  The root part of a plant—especially used of plants where a variety is grafted or budded onto a rootstock of known vigor and characteristic.

SEMIHARDY  A plant that can withstand fairly low temperatures, but needs protection from frost.

SEMIHARDY ANNUAL  An annual that is sown in gentle warmth in a greenhouse in spring, the seedlings being transferred to pots, then planted out once all risk of frost has passed.

SPECIES  An individual or group of plants, with common or similar characteristics, within a genus.

SPECIES ROSE  The term popularly used for a wild rose or one of its near-relatives.

SPORT  A plant that shows a marked and inheritable change from its parent. Often it is known as a mutation.

TUBER  A swollen, thickened, and fleshy stem or root. They serve as storage organs and help to perpetuate plants from one season to another.

VARIETY  see Cultivar.

# index

# hardiness zones map
# of North America

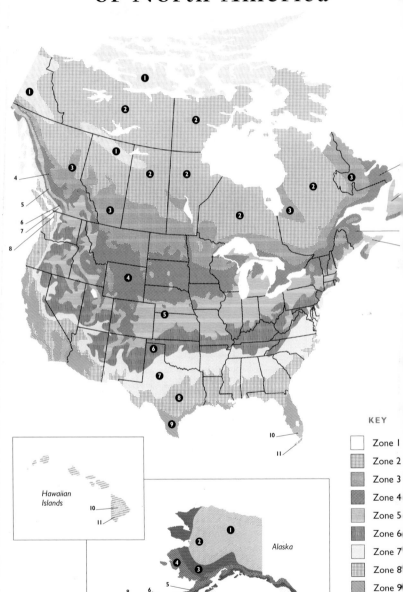

KEY

- ☐ Zone 1
- ▨ Zone 2
- ▨ Zone 3
- ▨ Zone 4
- ▨ Zone 5
- ▨ Zone 6
- ☐ Zone 7
- ▨ Zone 8
- ▨ Zone 9
- ▨ Zone 1
- ▨ Zone 1

*Hawaiian Islands*

*Alaska*